COLLEGE

– made –

EASY

MY PERSONAL TEXTBOOK OF HOW-TOS
AND DON'T-DOS OF COLLEGE

BY: TANNER MCFARLAND

First Printing, 2021

ISBN (Print) 978-1-7369875-9-9
ISBN (Ebook) 978-1-7369875-4-4

For bulk orders please contact trmcfarland96@gmail.com

Cover design and illustrations by Kaitlyn Hebden

www.tannermcfarland.com

Mom and Dad, your selfless acts of kindness have not gone unnoticed. Both of you have done so much good not only for our family, but for strangers who could never repay you. You give without expectation of getting anything in return. You inspire me everyday to become all that I can be, and to give to others in the same way that you do. You're the best parents ever.

Kathryn, the amount of support, love, and kindness you have given me over the years is difficult to put into words. You are always pushing me to new heights, challenging what I believe is possible. You make me a better person, a better man, and I know unquestionably you're always in my corner. I'm forever thankful for our life together.

To all who helped me on the journey of writing this book I thank you. It would not have been possible without you. Madison, Cody, Hillari, Kaitlyn, Andrew, Ralph, Carlos, Jeff, Tim, Jane, Hannah, Hayden, Team 003: Amy, Anna, Alex, Brad, Zach, John, Justin, Blake, Nathan, Chadd — You have all impacted me in unique ways. I'm grateful for the experiences we've had, our fruitful conversations, and friendships we share. My deepest and most sincere thank you.

— Tanner

table of CONTENTS

BEFORE WE START!

Before you even begin to crack open the pages of this book it's important to understand why you're reading it. What are you hoping to learn from this book? What are your biggest concerns about going to school? Before we get started I wanted to offer you the opportunity to get some of your thoughts out. At the end of the book, you'll be able to turn back to this page and re-address any of your thoughts or concerns from the beginning. Take a few moments and think about what you're worried about, what you have questions about, what you feel is missing, or any other thoughts you have about going to college. I promise you will get *way* more out of this book if you write some things down right here and now.

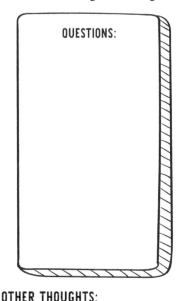

QUESTIONS:

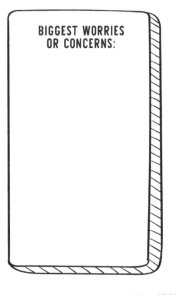

BIGGEST WORRIES
OR CONCERNS:

OTHER THOUGHTS:

_____

_____

_____

_____

Introduction :

DO WHAT YOU LOVE 👍

This first page is the beginning of your journey forward. I hope this book can be of service to you, give you comfort, shed some light on any anxious thoughts, and reassure you that you have what it takes!

Congratulations on taking the next step in your life; going to college! College isn't right for everyone, but I am glad to see that this is the path *you* chose. Whether you've just graduated high school and are beginning freshman year soon or you are already enrolled in college, this is the book for you. This is a guide I've developed through my college experience and the experiences of those around me. Everyone will experience college (and life!) differently, and how you make your way through college will be an adventure uncovered step by step. If you like some of the tips in this book and find them helpful, write them down, highlight them, keep them close, so that you'll remember them in the coming years. If you don't like some of the tips in this book, disregard them, they probably all won't be for you. Thanks for reading, let's dive in.

> FIND MEANING IN WHAT YOU DO. IF YOU LOVE WHAT YOU DO, YOU'VE WON THE GAME OF LIFE.

Do what you love. This needs to be stressed, then stressed again. You will see this recurring theme of doing what you love throughout the book. Being happy is the most important thing in life, so why do something if it doesn't make you happy? Listen I know you probably didn't love high school, and you may be thinking, "Why would I love college? There's classes and more homework, harder tests…" I understand (believe me, I do), I didn't love high school either, and there were plenty of aspects of college that were pretty terrible too (ever slept in a hallway because you're locked out of your room?). But it's important to focus on loving the outcome. College is pouring the foundation of a better life for you. Choose a major that you LOVE. This doesn't mean loving every single class, subject, or test (because you won't), but loving the idea of what you will get on the other side. Love the idea of being a doctor, an engineer, designer, teacher, writer, artist, or athletic trainer. Love the idea of the outcome.

If I am freaking you out a little because you don't know what you LOVE right now, then that's okay, you are not alone. Tons of people go through college and realize they don't know what they love. Don't worry, the solution to that is later in the book! This is a time to check out your options, see what you do and don't like and set yourself a solid foundation.

Having some foresight when it comes to college is crucial. You need to be a little more on top of things and realize this is the part of your life when what you do really matters. Sometimes that means you sacrifice current pleasure for something better later in life. It's called delayed gratification, and it's exactly what it sounds like. You put off gratification or enjoyment now, to get even more of it later. Relating to college, this means powering through those tough classes, knowing once they're done you will have your degree and be able to pursue whatever you want!

There has been plenty of research completed on delayed gratification, there's an interesting study showing how children respond to it. The short and sweet version of the study was this: Children were offered one marshmallow immediately, or two marshmallows if they could wait fifteen minutes. Some children ate the single marshmallow immediately and some stuck it out anxiously waiting for the second. Turns out, the children who chose to wait fifteen minutes for both marshmallows were more successful later in life. If you want more information on this, it's called The Marshmallow Experiment and was completed at Stanford in the 1960's by Walter Mischel. I'm telling you this because the next four years are going to kick you in the face. This book will soften the blow on a lot of things, but settle in for a rough ride. College is like waiting for the second marshmallow, if you're patient better things will come.

Okay, what specifically does that mean for you? It means keep your head up, there's going to be a lot (*a lot*) of work ahead of you to get where you want to go. Remember, if you're heading towards something you love then it will all be worth it, every second. Take the current pain and frustrations to achieve your goals and dreams as you grow. YOU get to decide what the future holds for yourself. All you need to do is decide. Ready to begin the journey? I just have one question for you: where do we start..?

Chapter One:

BEFORE SCHOOL

> ## SUCCESS IS THE CULMINATION OF COUNTLESS SMALL PREPARATIONS.

This chapter will take you through some of the necessary preparations to make sure you're ready to go when the time comes for school. There is a *lot* to do to prepare for school beforehand. Before we even get ready for school, have you decided on one? What should you look for in a school? What makes a good one, or a bad one? Does price matter? Or how big it is? What about location? All of these questions could be running through your head, and for good reason. Picking a college is a big decision, maybe even a scary one. But it's a decision *you* need to make.

The key to any venture is to know where you're going. If you don't know where you're going, how will you know when you get there? So, let's go over what to look for in a school. Picking a school is a really personal decision. It needs to come from you, what your preferences are and what is appealing to you. You're going to be spending a lot of time there, so take a moment to decide what's the absolute best for you. Some things to consider when looking for a school should include: location, price, programs, size, student to professor ratio, male to female ratio, reviews of the school, the program structure, and financial aid just to name a few.

I can't tell you what is best, what makes you most comfortable, or what makes the most sense for you. Look at these aspects and decide for yourself what is most important and what makes you feel best. This is a crucial point in life and you need to do some research before making the big decision. If, by chance, you make the wrong choice and end up at the wrong school or in the wrong major there are plenty of options that we will get to later. Get excited to look into schools, this is a tremendous time in your life, there's so much to be stoked about.

If you're wondering about the best time to apply to schools, usually the beginning of senior year in highschool is the sweet spot. A lot of colleges require applications to be submitted starting in January, so if you start applying around September of your senior year you should be safe. Check into the schools you're interested in to find their specific deadlines though. Once those applications start flying and get submitted, you begin the waiting game. The waiting could be filled with anxiety, but it won't last long, most often colleges will get back to you with their decision in the March-April timeframe.

Applications to each school will be a little different. It's important you fill out the Common App found at www.commonapp.org. The vast majority of schools accept the Common App, saving you from doing an entire application for each school. Some colleges may have additional requirements, but the Common App will save you loads of time for many schools. It's incredibly easy to do on your own time and submitting it to whatever schools you want is a breeze.

You should also take some time to prepare a college essay. This is an essay where you can show your voice and personality. The Common App and your transcript will show who you are on paper, but the essay will allow you to speak directly to the admissions office. Take some time and put some solid effort into this, really make it your own. College Board has some great resources on how to get started with your essay if you're unsure. Check out www.collegeboard.org for more information. There are a lot of different things you can talk about in your college essay, but it's supposed to help you stand out. I suggest using it to talk about your life experience thus far, and where you're hoping to go in life. Be your authentic self and show your passion. Alright, now that we have that covered, I'm going to assume you're a little further along and have already applied to schools, so let's keep moving forward.

Next, once you hear back from all the schools you applied to, take a look at their financial aid packages (and turn to Chapter 4), and then the decision becomes yours. Something I want to nip in the bud right now, if college isn't for you, or all the schools you apply to deny you (unlikely) - that's *not* the end of the road. There are always options, you can continue to search for schools, community colleges, online programs, trade schools, or begin working in a field you already know you like. If you don't get into your first choice, remember things happen for a reason. Maybe you weren't meant to go there. You'll look back in a few years and see why, trust me here. Wentworth Institute of Technology wasn't my first choice. I got rejected by my first choice, and wait-listed (and eventually rejected) by my second choice. So, I've been there and it'll all work out great. Looking back I wouldn't change a single thing.

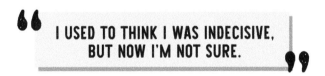

I USED TO THINK I WAS INDECISIVE, BUT NOW I'M NOT SURE.

Even if you have selected what school you're attending, read this section! You might just stumble across something useful. It's a good idea to take a tour of prospective colleges you're looking into. If you've already selected where you want to go, that's great! I still suggest taking a tour, maybe even multiple tours before move in day. You want to feel comfortable at school and tours will help you find the big ticket items like dorms, the cafe, library, and academic buildings you're going to have classes in. It's super easy to set up a tour of any college. Their admissions office will have posted on their website how to schedule a tour that fits what you're interested in seeing. Some can be general campus tours, they can be geared towards athletics, or even a specific program.

If you have trouble finding tour reservations online, give the schools admissions office a call and set one up over the phone. Most colleges will have you sign up for a group tour, you and other students will all follow a staff member around to see the sights. You may also have the option to set up a private tour. This would be just you/your family and the staff member. It's a little more personal and you may be able to see more of what you actually want to see. However, going with other students may be a good idea because they might ask questions you hadn't even thought of. Whatever you choose, I think tours are important. You could also get some free swag, who doesn't love a free t-shirt or water bottle?

In short, there's a lot of change happening when you're first moving to school. The last thing you want on top of all that stress is to have no idea where to even go for food. Touring schools will help you decide on a college and allow you to get your bearings before day one.

THERE'S A DAY MADE IN YOUR HONOR

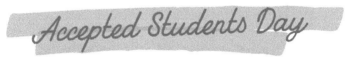

If you've been accepted to a college already, congratulations! One great thing most colleges do for accepted students is hold a day specifically for them. Accepted students day is meant for all new students to come and see campus, hopefully for a second time because you went on a tour! On this day students can see their program more in depth, maybe take a tour of the academic buildings, get a free lunch, meet some faculty and, finally, they will try to sell you their school if you haven't already committed.

You can attend accepted students day without committing to a school. It's an opportunity for them to show off a little and flex all the great things about their school. You may still need to decide on a school and this could be the deciding factor. If you have already committed, definitely still go to accepted students day.

After accepted students day, closer to the beginning of the year, is orientation. A little less fun and more business for this one. Orientation is only for students who have confirmed enrollment. This is when you will see the dorms and possibly even the room you will be staying in. You'll get more detail about where everything is on campus, the facilities, safety, meal cards and IDs, housing, and more. They want to make sure you know what's going on when you get there for your first day. Some schools hold orientation in the summer a few weeks before you move in, others have you move in a week or so early and have a week-long orientation before classes start. Either way, it's a great time for questions and to get a sense of direction before the mayhem of classes start.

Connecting with some of the other students on accepted students day or during orientation can really help you feel more comfortable once you're on campus for good. You can also find other students via social media before move in day. A few familiar faces during the first days of school will really curb any anxiety you're feeling about all the newness that comes with heading to school.

KEEP CALM, AND SHOP ON.

Another "to-do list" item to complete during the summer before you head off to some of the most unforgettable years of your life - you need to go shopping. Oh yeah, shopping! On the next few pages I have a sizable list of items you may need for the upcoming years. These items are not only important for school, but can also make you feel at home. There's no reason you can't have fun shopping for college, so make a day of it. It's really great to have a blank canvas of a room and have the opportunity to design it for yourself. There's a lot of items on the list you're going to need, some will be fun to pick out and some of them are not going to be so fun to buy - like a powerstrip (who *wants* to buy a powerstrip?). Most items you'll be able to shop around for and find a style that suits you and really personalizes your space. Have fun with it, and the earlier you shop the easier time you'll have getting what you want and need!

Chapter Two:

PACKING

Let's get right into it. What do you need for college? If you're commuting to school then you've got it a bit easier than the kids moving away from home, so we will start with you. Kids moving into school: take note here as well. School supplies! This isnt grade school where you need to go buy dinosaur erasers and fabric book covers (although some people still buy them trust me). Like most things, being over prepared is better than being underprepared. Ever hear someone say, "Proper planning prevents poor performance" or something to that nature? The "Five P's for success?" Well, they're right.

The first essential thing you will need is a laptop. You don't need to go out and get the most expensive crazy laptop there is, but technology is advancing so rapidly that almost every class uses laptops in some capacity. Get something you, or Mom and Dad, can afford. Don't be embarrassed if you don't have the newest or most expensive Mac or PC, everyone is too concerned with themselves anyways. Realistically, with the applications you'll likely use in school, the most basic laptops will perform just as well. Being an engineer and business student, I'm partial to PCs. I've used both Lenovo and Dell laptops and love them, but there are many brands and models that will get the job done. The next items are more common, so get what suits you best:

○ LAPTOP _____

○ NOTEBOOKS _____

○ PENS & PENCILS _____

○ BACKPACK _____

○ WATER BOTTLE _____

○ EXTRA PHONE CORD _____

○ BATTERY PACK

○ BINDERS _____

○ CALCULATORS _____
"SCIENTIFIC, ANYTHING TEXAS INSTRUMENTS WILL DO, BUT LOOK INTO THE FUNCTIONALITIES YOU WILL/WON'T NEED"

○ WALLET _____

○ HEADPHONES _____

○ EXTERNAL HARD/FLASH DRIVE

MOST LIVING ITEMS LIKE CLOTHES, TOILETRIES AND ALL OF THAT STUFF WILL BE LEFT AT HOME FOR COMMUTERS. THE LIST ABOVE IS PROBABLY INCOMPLETE SO IF YOU THINK OF ANYTHING ELSE WHILE READING, SCRIBBLE THEM DOWN HERE AND FIND THIS PAGE WHEN IT'S TIME TO SHOP OR PACK. IF I REALLY FORGOT SOME STUFF, THROW SOME ITEMS IN THE MARGINS!

_____

_____

_____

_____

Here is a more comprehensive list for those of you who are moving into school. Check the boxes when you have collected the item, and there is room at the end for you to add anything else you need! You can also head on over to www.tannermcfarland.com/extras to download this complete packing guide!

THE COLLEGE MADE EASY
ultimate packing guide

Room supplies

- [ ] ROOM/DESK LAMP
- [ ] SMALL TRASH CAN/BAGS
- [ ] STORAGE BINS
- [ ] FAN (¡MUY IMPORTANTE!)
- [ ] BULLETIN BOARD/ PINS
- [ ] CALENDAR
- [ ] LIGHT STRIPS OR DECORATIVE LIGHTING

- [ ] COMMAND STRIPS OR DOUBLE SIDED HANGING TAPE
- [ ] SMALL TOOLKIT WITH 3-5 BAISC TOOLS
- [ ] COMFY DESK CHAIR
- [ ] BED RISERS (ALLOW FOR EXTRA STORAGE UNDER BED)
- [ ] SHOE RACK
- [ ] PICTURES/DECOR

Laundry

- ☐ PILLOWS
- ☐ PILLOWCASES
- ☐ BLANKETS
- ☐ TOWELS
- ☐ FACE CLOTHS
- ☐ CLOTHES HANGERS
- ☐ LINT BRUSH
- ☐ SHEETS (CHECK WITH SCHOOL ON BED SIZE. TYPICALLY TWIN EXTRA LONG)
- ☐ LAUNDRY BASKET
- ☐ LAUNDRY DETERGENT
- ☐ DRYER SHEETS
- ☐ STAIN REMOVER OR TIDE TO-GO

Desk Supplies

- ☐ HIGHLIGHTERS
- ☐ STAPLER/STAPLES
- ☐ PLANNER
- ☐ SCIENTIFIC CALCULATOR
- ☐ PRINTER *OPTIONAL
- ☐ PRINTER PAPER *OPTIONAL
- ☐ PENS & PENCILS
- ☐ USB FLASH DRIVE/ EXTERNAL DRIVE
- ☐ PERMANENT MARKERS
- ☐ NOTEBOOKS (I SUGGEST 5 SUBJECT)
- ☐ 3" X 5" INDEX CARDS
- ☐ STICKY NOTES
- ☐ PAPER & BINDER CLIPS

Electronics

- [ ] LAPTOP/CHARGER
- [ ] PORTABLE SPEAKER
- [ ] HDMI CORD
- [ ] ETHERNET CORD
- [ ] ROUTER (IF ALLOWED)
- [ ] SURGE PROTECTOR
- [ ] EXTENSION CORD
- [ ] POWER STRIP (DORM ROOMS NEVER HAVE ENOUGH OUTLETS)
- [ ] HEADPHONES

Toiletries

- [ ] ANTACID
- [ ] PAIN RELIEVERS
- [ ] VITAMINS
- [ ] DECONGESTANTS & FEVER REDUCERS
- [ ] BANDAGES
- [ ] COUGH DROPS
- [ ] SHOWER CADDY
- [ ] SACRIFICIAL FLIP FLOPS FOR SHOWER SHOES
- [ ] BODY WASH, SHAMPOO, & CONDITIONER
- [ ] HAIRSTYLING PRODUCTS
- [ ] HAIR DRIER, CURLER, STRAIGHTENER
- [ ] TOOTHPASTE/ TOOTHBRUSH
- [ ] MOUTHWASH
- [ ] FLOSS
- [ ] BRUSHES/COMBS
- [ ] TWEEZERS
- [ ] NAIL CLIPPERS/ FILE
- [ ] RAZOR/SHAVING CREAM

Toiletries (cont)

- [ ] LOTION
- [ ] COTTON SWABS
- [ ] PLUNGER (IF YOU'RE IN A SUITE-STYLE ROOM)

- [ ] DEODORANT
- [ ] PERFUME OR COLOGNE

Clothing

- [ ] SOCKS
- [ ] PANTS
- [ ] JEANS
- [ ] PERSONALS
- [ ] SWEATERS/SWEATSHIRTS
- [ ] SWEATPANTS
- [ ] PAJAMAS
- [ ] SLIPPERS
- [ ] LIGHT AND HEAVY JACKET
- [ ] GLOVES, SCARF, HAT

- [ ] BASEBALL CAP
- [ ] SNEAKERS, BOOTS, FLIP FLOPS
- [ ] AT LEAST 1 PAIR OF DRESS SHOES
- [ ] AT LEAST ONE BUSINESS CASUAL OUTFIT
- [ ] DRESS
- [ ] SWIMSUIT
- [ ] HANGERS FOR CLOSET
- [ ] SHIRTS (DON'T BRING EVERY T-SHIRT YOU OWN)

Household Items

- [ ] TRASH BAGS
- [ ] PAPER TOWELS
- [ ] ALL PURPOSE CLEANER
- [ ] PLASTIC STORAGE BAGS
- [ ] TUPPERWARE
- [ ] DISH SOAP
- [ ] SPONGE/DISH BRUSH
- [ ] DISINFECTANT WIPES

- [ ] TISSUES
- [ ] BOWLS, PLATES, CUPS
- [ ] MUG(S)
- [ ] WATER FILER (BRITA)
- [ ] UTENSILS
- [ ] TRAVEL MUG
- [ ] WATER BOTTLES
- [ ] SILVERWARE

Odds and Ends

- [ ] BACKPACK
- [ ] SPORTS EQUIPMENT
- [ ] GYM BAG
- [ ] TOTE BAG
- [ ] SMALL HANDHELD VACUUM

- [ ] BICYCLE, HELMET, LOCK
- [ ] SKATEBOARD OR ROLLER BLADES
- [ ] BRING SNACKS TO GET YOU STARTED UNTIL YOU FIGURE EVERYTHING OUT!
- [ ] UMBRELLA

Shared Items

TALK WITH ROOMMATES BEFOREHAND SO YOU
DON'T END UP WITH REDUNDANT ITEMS!

☐ SPEAKERS

☐ TV

☐ COFFEE MACHINE (IF ALLOWED)

☐ MICROWAVE (IF ALLOWED)

☐ MINI FRIDGE

☐ RUG

☐ POSTERS OR WALL DECOR

ADD ANYTHING I FORGOT OR ANYTHING EXTRA YOU WILL NEED HERE:

☐ _____

☐ _____

☐ _____

☐ _____

☐ _____

☐ _____

☐ _____

☐ _____

☐ _____

☐ _____

☐ _____

☐ _____

☐ _____

☐ _____

One thing people may forget when packing, and something they would love to have no matter how far away from home they go, is a reminder of home. Bring something to remind you of home or of your parents. A picture is awesome, a note they've written to you, a special gift they've given you, something to that effect. You'll appreciate it everyday, being reminded of where you're from and the people who care for you. Something else you should bring, not only to college but everywhere you go, is the intangible love and support of people in your life. It might sound cheesy but regardless of distance or time, there are people who deeply care about you. Pack that away somewhere you won't lose it. Bring it to the forefront of your mind during tough times no matter what they may be. Remember that whatever happens these people love and care about you, that will make it a bit better for you, trust me. And don't forget, regularly calling family and friends is the easiest way to stay in touch, catch up, and remain connected.

When you move to school remember that you're not only moving *into* school, you're moving *out of* home. It's a big event for your parents too, you're leaving the nest. Your mom or dad may want to make your bed, make sure your bathroom is set up, or something else. Let them. While this is an exciting new chapter in your life, your parents have been thinking about the day you leave the nest for eighteen years. Go easy on them, they're doing it because they care and will miss you. They want everything to be all set up for you, just like home. They want it to be a smooth transition for you and it's how they show they love you. Once you're all moved in, and it's time for them to leave, give them a big hug like when Michael Ohr goes to college in *The Blind Side*. Also, don't try to act cool and like you don't care about your parents and just shoo them out. You're not cool if you're going to just kick them out without saying thank you and showing them some love. It's much more cool to be thankful and appreciative of them. Remember all the things they've done for you and given you in this life. Let's talk about move in day logistics before it's time to say "see you later" and step into this new chapter of your life. So, here we are, it's time for college, buckle down and let's do it.

Chapter Three:

MOVE IN DAY

> ❝ IN ORDER TO FLY, YOU
> MUST LEAVE THE NEST. ❞

It's here. Today is the day you've been thinking about all summer, possibly dreading, possibly bursting with excitement. Ready or not, it's here. It's move in day at college. Now you've probably seen movies or clips of stressful move in days, and they're mostly accurate. It's a day filled with stress, confusion, lots of walking, rushing, happiness, sadness, excitement, newness, and all kinds of highs and lows. You will have a ton of places to be, and potentially not know where any of them are. One thing I can guarantee is this; you will figure it out, and make it through. There's a lot to think about on move in day, so I will outline some things you should keep in mind and also give you a rough outline of what the day may hold.

First, you're going to feel all sorts of emotions. And your parents are too. Sadness that you're leaving your parents, excited for the new place and to be on your own, scared to find new friends and start classes, nervous to share a room with someone you barely know, the list goes on. There's no question there is a lot going on on move in day. My advice here? Just be in the moment. Feel those feelings, don't bury them. Going to college is emotional, you can't escape that. It is for everyone. But the emotional whirlwind won't last forever, you'll settle in pretty quickly. Let's talk about the actual day now.

Before even setting off for the day, remember that before unloading your car at school you need to load your car at home. Think about how to pack the car so it will be easy to unload on the other end when you arrive at school. If you packed the car in an organized manner, unloading will be a breeze. You should also absolutely do some research prior to arrival. Your school should hopefully send you some information about move in day, but they might not include everything I'm going to talk about. One of my biggest pet peeves is to drive somewhere and when I arrive, not know where to park. I hate driving around aimlessly asking myself "Can I fit there?" or "Is that metered?"' or "There's no 'no parking' sign so that's fine..? Right?" Do yourself a favor and confirm where you will be parking, maybe Google Map it so you can see it before you get there. You probably have to check in before you can do anything at all so the school knows who is on campus. So after parking, this is step one. Next you need to know where to get your ID. You'll need your ID and/or keys to get into your building.

There also may be upperclassmen there to help you move in! Pretty cool perk to get other people to wheel all your crap to your room! Although, I would caution you to make sure anything of value or fragility is carried by you or a family member, just for safety's sake. Schools may have large wheeled bins to put your stuff in, but if you have a dolly I would say it wouldn't hurt to bring it. Another tip, when you've brought everything to your room and are bringing suitcases and bags back to the car, leave a small suitcase or duffle bag at school. You'll need something to stuff all your dirty laundry into when you go home on the occasional weekend, it'll come in handy.

Accept early on that move in day is going to be quite a long day. Probably getting up early to leave home, a decent drive, unloading and getting all set up. It will be especially long for your parents if they are the ones who bring you. Take an extra moment to say thank you. Like I said earlier, it's not only move in day, but it's also move out day from your house. This is significant for you *and* for them. Before you go, if you wanted to really make them happy, write them a letter and stash it somewhere around the house. Then in a few weeks text them and tell them where it is. They'll love to have a handwritten note from you and, maybe, it'll prompt them to send you a care package - who knows!

One huge piece of advice I can give is for clothes that will be hung up. Here is the best way to pack them: first leave them on the hangers, hung up in your closet at home. Then take a new forty gallon trash bag and pull it over ten to twenty items from the bottom up, tying the top of the bag off with the top of the hanger still sticking out on top. Check out the images below.

When you get to the dorm you can hang the big bag of clothes on the rack using the exposed hangers, rip or cut the bag off of the clothes, and boom you're done! Less wrinkles, and more importantly less headache with tangled hangers and folding and all that crap.

For these small items I used a thirteen gallon trash bag, but I would suggest getting either thirty or forty gallon bags. While I got fifteen items into this small bag, the forty gallon bags will allow you to be able to fit more clothes and not risk them getting wrinkled at the bottom of the bag. Also, I suggest using white bags so you can see what is inside in case you want to organize faster once you're at school! Shout out to my girlfriend for letting me use her closet for these photos!

Here's another pro tip: bring either a doorstop or something to prop the door open. You're going to be making many trips in and out of your room and needing the key to open the door thirty times will get old. Avoid the temptation to dress super nice, you may get a little dirty and can always change once everything is put away. It's not a bad idea to be prepared with some drinks and snacks, too. Take some breaks when you need, it doesn't need to be all go-go-go. You may have the same move in time as your roommate(s) so plan for this as well. It will be stressful enough for you and your family to get in and out of there with all your stuff. But imagine multiple people doing this in a shoebox of a room all at once. Talk about tight spaces. Whatever your expectations are, make sure they are not for the day to go perfectly. You may forget things, realize you packed too much or too little, feel rushed or stressed, or feel a range of crazy emotions. That's okay. You are not alone in feeling this way. Everything will get sorted out and you'll be just fine.

Finally, the room is set up, and it's time for parents to go. There may be crying, there certainly was when I moved in freshman year. Maybe try to schedule a time to be done unpacking and for them to head home so the goodbye doesn't drag on longer than it needs to, and no one's driving home at 3 AM. Maybe plan to grab a bite to eat together after the room is set up and then say goodbyes from there. In this day and age with Facetime and texting, you can stay in pretty close contact. Almost anyone you want to talk to is only a call or text away which should give you some comfort. When they're leaving, it's time to be thankful that you made it here. Wave goodbye to your parents, a new chapter is just beginning. Reality is about to set in, you're in college, my friend.

Chapter Four:

💰 MONEY

> **YOU EITHER MASTER MONEY, OR, ON SOME LEVEL, MONEY MASTERS YOU.**
>
> —TONY ROBBINS

Here's a fun part, I did a little research into what questions students had going into college. I found there were quite a few questions about money, so here are my two cents. See what I did there...? I'm sure you've heard all the sayings about broke college kids, how they eat Ramen for every meal and steal toilet paper from the bathrooms around campus (trust me, it's been done). Well, you may not have to go to those extremes, but college can get pretty expensive. Sidenote, anyone out there who genuinely likes Ramen and you're like "Eating Ramen for every meal, what, is that a challenge?" Please do not take it upon yourself to eat Ramen for every meal.

Anyway, everyone's money situation is different and how you manage your expenses is your business and your business alone. But! Know once you make decisions, you have to live with the consequences. That's a tough lesson to learn, but once you make that connection, you begin to be more responsible with your choices. That means you have to own the way you spend money. If you spend all your cash and need to eat light for a week or can't go out with friends, you need to own that it was *your* poor money decisions that got you there. It's no one's fault but your own. Be really intentional about how you spend/save money in college. It can really have an impact on how your life after college starts.

Don't expect to be rich in college because it's probably not going to happen. But at the same time, you won't be standing outside the cafeteria starving, asking people for meal dollars either. One lesson I've learned, and you're going to think to yourself, "Well I already knew that" is this: money goes out a lot faster than it comes in. I'll say that again, *money goes out a lot faster than it comes in.*

Hear me out here. Look at what you make per hour at any job you've had. Now think about going out and spending $75 with your friends once or twice a week. That's not *too* much money. But think about how many hours you needed to spend at work earning that money. If you make $10 an hour, *that's seven and a half hours of your life.* Is that worth it? Decide for yourself! If you work an hourly job you don't really pay for things with money, you pay for them with hours of your life.

Feeling broke or tight on money is really uncomfortable, I've experienced it and I'm sure if you haven't, you will at some point. But remember, it doesn't last forever. After college you'll get a real job and be making real money. And, for the time being you don't need to remain broke. Find an on campus job or somewhere near campus to pick up some hours. Take a hard look at your spending habits and maybe try saying "No" more. Also, you don't need to spend money to have fun. That's a hard truth a lot of young people have a difficult time understanding, but it's true. There are a ton of fun things to do that are free, you just need to be creative. Check out some examples on the next page.

- MOVIE MARATHON
- TAKE PHOTOS FOR YOUR INSTAGRAM
- FEED SOME DUCKS
- LAY ON THE BEACH
- BOARD GAMES
- LOOK AT THE STARS
- TRANSFORM YOUR DORM ROOM
- TAKE YOUR LAPTOP AND WATCH A MOVIE OUTSIDE
- DING-DONG-DITCH YOUR FLOOR MATES
- IF YOU'RE CREATIVE ENOUGH, THERE'S PLENTY MORE!

- WATCH A MOVIE
- READ A BOOK
- GO EXPLORE A PARK
- FIND A WATERFALL
- WALK DOWNTOWN
- CREATE A PHOTOSHOOT
- GO TO A SPORTS GAME
- FIND A NEW CLUB
- GO ON A HIKE
- VISIT A MUSEUM

Last note here. One of the best lessons I've learned about money is not to spend it on stuff that you don't need, to impress people you don't even like. People are way too caught up on having the newest clothes, cars, water bottles and this and that. Why? To impress people. People they don't even like! The people who you should surround yourself with don't care if your clothes are a year old or what you drive. If you're buying items to impress people or to look good on social media, you lose. Simple as that. Don't buy sh*t you don't need to make it seem like you're rich. It's not worth it and will only hurt you in the long run.

" I CAN'T WAIT TO FILL OUT THE FAFSA!

-NO ONE EVER "

Okay, we covered pocket money, but let's get into some real money talk, financial aid and student loans. When it comes to paying for school you have some options. Go to www.tannermcfarland.com/extras for a one stop shop of all the links and references mentioned in this section. Loans are a pretty hot topic right now and paying them back is something everyone dreads.

It's somewhat of an abstract concept at your age, or at least it was for me. In my case, I was taking out loans that were more money than I had made in my whole life. I couldn't *really* wrap my head around what was happening. I felt rich if I had a couple hundred bucks to my name, so tens of thousands of dollars being thrown here and there didn't even make sense to me. I feel high school and society has done you and me a disservice. There isn't nearly enough education about loans and different ways to pay for school. It's vitally important for you to understand how paying for school works, because it's a lot of money and you don't want to make poor decisions that will negatively impact your young adult life. Depending on who you ask, there are a variety of ways you can pay for school. Some people's parents can front a check and pay off tuition with the stroke of a pen. Other people may need student loans to cover the cost. There are also scholarships you can apply for to help cover the cost. The options go on and on. If paying for school is a large concern for you, take some time to learn about available resources and you'll find there are more ways than you think. While I don't know every loan, scholarship, or method out there to pay for school, I can talk about my experience so you can learn through me.

So how does financial aid from schools work? Financial aid as a whole can seem complex, probably because it is. I will do my best to give you the most important information in an easy to follow guide so you can navigate the world of financial aid. Take it slow and if you need to write some notes in the margins or go over this chapter a few times, please do so.

Also please note this is not financial advice and you should consult with a professional about your specific situation. My lawyer made me say that. Just kidding. But you really should talk to your shool's financial services office, or maybe even your high school guidance counsellor, about all of your options before making any decisions you aren't sure of.

I made the flowchart below to lay out the big picture of financial aid. The remainder of the chapter will follow this flowchart step by step and I will expand on each of the topics so you can understand the major concepts. I probably sound like a broken record, but it really is important you understand financial aid. Loan payments can take a big chunk of your paycheck well into your thirty's if you aren't diligent. Let's jump in and work things out.

FINANCIAL AID PATHWAY:

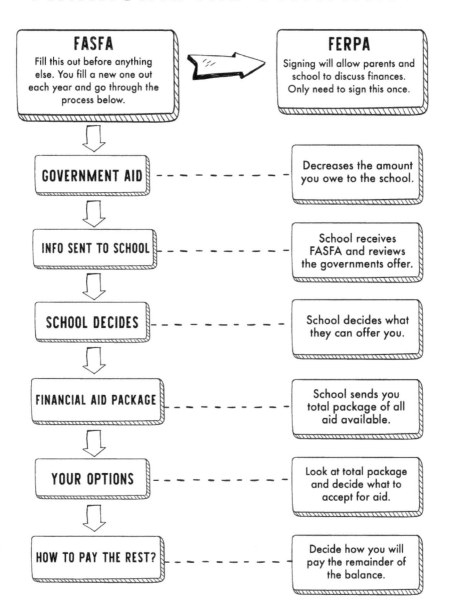

FASFA
Fill this out before anything else. You fill a new one out each year and go through the process below.

FERPA
Signing will allow parents and school to discuss finances. Only need to sign this once.

GOVERNMENT AID — Decreases the amount you owe to the school.

INFO SENT TO SCHOOL — School receives FASFA and reviews the governments offer.

SCHOOL DECIDES — School decides what they can offer you.

FINANCIAL AID PACKAGE — School sends you total package of all aid available.

YOUR OPTIONS — Look at total package and decide what to accept for aid.

HOW TO PAY THE REST? — Decide how you will pay the remainder of the balance.

FAFSA

First things first, we need to talk about the FAFSA. It stands for the Free Application for Federal Student Aid. It's a simple application you need to fill out to be able to receive financial aid from the government. Do a quick Google search or go to www.studentaid.gov and you can find the FAFSA and fill it out online. You need to fill the FAFSA out <u>every year</u> for school. Your financial situation can change from year to year, so a new FAFSA is needed. The federal government uses the FAFSA to determine how much aid they will give you based on you and your parent's financial situation. Have your parent's financial information ready when filling this out too. The government determines what they expect you to pay for school based on how much money you and your family make, and then gives you aid based on that.

When you're filling out the FAFSA you get to choose what schools you want your information sent to. These are the schools you're going to apply to, or have applied to. This way, once the government decides what they will give you for aid they tell the schools you have selected what you will receive for federal assistance. The schools then take a look at what the government will give you, and they look at your FAFSA too, and then finally decide what they are going to give you for assistance. This is known as your financial aid package.

Government Aid

The FAFSA is also used to determine what government aid you are eligible for, like loans and grants. If you have been accepted to a college, chances are you will get some type of aid from the federal government just for submitting the FAFSA. You may be eligible for both subsidized and unsubsidized federal loans. Basically all you need to know is that you will <u>pay less over time using a subsidized loan</u> rather than an unsubsidized loan. Also, quick note on federal loans: if you need loans, it's usually a good idea to take all federal loans first over bank loans. Federal loans have a much lower interest rate than the private loans you would get from a bank. A few percentage points on the interest you pay might not seem like much but trust me, there can be thousands of dollars of difference for a single percentage point.

Another type of aid you may be eligible for based on your unique situation is called a Pell Grant. This is a grant (meaning it doesn't need to be paid back) from the government. It will be shown in your financial aid package if you are eligible to receive it. You don't need to do anything more than fill out the FAFSA to be considered for a Pell Grant. You can choose to accept it or not, but it's as close to free money as you're ever going to get so I wanted to make sure I mentioned it!

Information Sent To Schools

Once the government decides what they will offer you, they send that information to each school you have selected. Whatever loans, Pell Grants, and other aid they are offering is sent to each school you are applying to. The schools will already have your FAFSA and now have all the information they need for aid purposes. Next they will decide what they will offer you.

School Decides

Each of the schools you apply to will take a look at your FAFSA and the government aid you are offered and decide for themselves what they are going to offer you. Schools can also give aid based on things that are not included in the FAFSA such as sports scholarships, academic scholarships, and others. Once each school decides what they are going to give you they will provide you with a financial aid package which outlines what you're eligible for and ultimately what it's going to cost you to attend. Sometimes it takes a little while for them to process everything so the time after you submit your FAFSA can be an anxious time. My advice here is wait for each school to send you their package before deciding where to go. Aid can vary widely from school to school and you want to make sure you're getting the best deal at the best school. Alright, so what would a financial aid package look like?

Financial Aid Package

Like I said, you will get a financial aid package from every school you apply to and it will include what the government is offering you and what the school is offering you. Each school is independent when it comes to how they decide to offer aid. Some schools will offer you none, and others may offer you quite a bit of aid. In each school's offering, the amount the government is giving you will stay the same. What changes is the amount each individual school will offer you. Some schools offer different amounts of aid based on major and some also offer merit based scholarships that are related to your grades. Wait and see what schools give you and weigh your options accordingly. Also, schools do not usually negotiate financial aid, what you get is what you get.

If you have questions about anything financial aid related, call the financial aid office at any of the schools you have applied to. They can explain how it all works, how to apply to scholarships, fill out the FAFSA or FERPA, where to find additional aid, and answer any other questions you have. Whatever you have questions about, the financial aid office has heard the same exact question a thousand times before. It's their job to know the answer and to help you. In the end, colleges want your money so they will work hard to help you understand and attend their school! Okay, let's take a look at a simple example of a student aid package so you can understand how everything fits together.

Financial Aid Package Example

COST OF ATTENDANCE

TUITION (THIS GOES TOWARDS ROOM AND BOARD, AND THE COST FOR ALL THE COURSES YOU TAKE)	$32,000
FEES (FOR LABS, TECH, ORIENTATION, TRANSPORATION, ETC.)	$4,000
TOTAL COST THE TOTAL COST OF ATTENDING THE SCHOOL PER YEAR	$36,000

FINANCIAL AID PACKAGE

FEDERAL PELL GRANT	$4,500
FEDERAL DIRECT SUBSIDIZED LOAN	$3,000
FEDERAL DIRECT UNSUBSIDIZED LOAN	$2,500
UNIVERSITY SCHOLARSHIP	$4,000
WORK STUDY*	$5,000 *DOES NOT LOWER AMOUNT DUE
TOTAL AID THE TOTAL AMOUNT OF AID THAT LOWERS WHAT IS DUE AT THE BEGINNING OF EACH YEAR DON'T FORGET- THIS ISN'T ALL FREE MONEY, LOANS AND SOME SCHOLARSHIPS NEED TO BE PAID BACK IN THE FUTURE!	$14,000
TOTAL COST - TOTAL AID	$36,000 - $14,000 =
EXPECTED COST THIS IS WHAT YOU ARE RESPONSIBLE FOR PAYING OUT OF POCKET. YOU CAN COVER THIS COST USING ONE OR MORE OF THE FOLLOWING: PARENT PLUS LOAN, BANK LOAN, SCHOLARSHIPS, PAYMENT PLAN TO SCHOOL, PAY FROM YOUR SAVINGS, PARENTS/FAMILY WRITE CHECK, WORK STUDY.	$22,000

In this example, school costs a total of $36,000 to attend. Next is what you are offered as a financial aid package, which totals $14,000 (the $5,000 for work study does not lower your bill, we will cover this soon, keep reading). This leaves $22,000 for you to cover. Let's look at your options first, then we will figure out how to pay the $22,000.

Your Options

You have the option to accept or deny any aid that is offered to you. In my experience, aid like Pell Grants are usually smart to accept because they don't need to be paid back. Loans can get a little confusing because of interest rates and how they are paid to your school. But remember, subsidized loans are typically cheaper than unsubsidized because the way interest works. You can also accept both types like the example above. The smartest thing to do here is to see what aid you're given, call the financial aid office with any questions you have, and decide what is best for you. Although, I do believe it's typical for people to accept all the aid they're given (it's less you need to pay out of pocket now and for some that can be the difference of attending school or not), but the choice is yours.

How To Pay The Rest?

Free money is the best kind of money! Scholarships are awesome because they are literally free money. The worst part of student loans is having to pay them back. Scholarships, you do not need to pay back! What other motivation do you need to find some? Start to look for some by going to your high school guidance counsellor. They will have a ton of local scholarships for you to apply for. These can range from a hundred dollars to a few thousand dollars. You can find additional scholarships online for your unique interests and talents as well. There are scholarships out there for almost anything. You will probably cruise right through this section and tell yourself you'll find some later. But you really should force yourself to get started finding some. Isn't a few hours on your computer worth a couple hundred bucks?

While we're on this topic, you can start right here! I started the College Made Easy Scholarship to help <u>you</u> pay for school! Go to www.tannermcfarland.com/scholarship to apply. I made the application super simple and the money will be sent directly to your school. Head to my website to see if you qualify and get some FREE money! Someone's going to win this scholarship, take a couple minutes and see if it could be you!

Scholarships are something you need to apply for, usually in the form of a questionnaire and/or essay. From there a board or individual will go through the application and choose a winner. Scholarships are so underrated, because if you receive enough they can really add up! Some students have received so many that they paid their whole tuition! Imagine going to school for free because of the scholarship money you've received.

Make sure you follow the directions *exactly* when filling out scholarship applications *and* make the deadline. They're offering you a huge financial opportunity, if you don't follow their rules you'll just be wasting your time. Some scholarships can be applied for each year, others are one time only or year dependent. Once enrolled at a school there may be more scholarships you qualify for (like being in a specific major), so look for scholarships all throughout school. Once at college, talk to the financial aid office, they will have a litany of scholarship information for you.

A quick example illustrating why you should apply for scholarships is this: My mom worked as part of a board for our local youth soccer organization. Each year they have a scholarship to give to a high school senior that is on their way to college. To be eligible, you are just required to write a short essay and submit it by the due date. One year, they received *zero* applications. No one applied! They had free money to give away, anyone could have gotten it, but not a single person took the time to look into it and submit an application. Someone could have taken forty five minutes to write the essay and received hundreds of dollars by default because they would have been the only applicant. Moral of the story, apply to as many as you can. You never know how many people submit applications and in case I haven't said it enough… it's free money, it makes a difference.

Work study job? Study while you work!

Work study jobs are a great way to make a little extra cash while you are in school. I included work study in this section because some people are awarded work study but don't use it. It's not used as much as other aid because you actually have to work for it. If you're eligible schools will offer you an amount of money for work study, say $5,000. As I mentioned earlier, this *does not* lower the amount you owe the school. Instead, you need to apply for and be hired for a work study position at the school. Then, you work and get paid an hourly wage, say $20 an hour, until you have earned $5,000. So, for this example that would be 250 hours over a semester which comes out to be just under sixteen hours per week. The reason it's included in your financial aid package is because the thought is you will use the money you earn to pay for school. Now, this isn't always what happens, I certainly didn't use the money I earned to pay for school. Looking back that probably would have been the smart thing to do and I would encourage you to, but you certainly don't *have* to use it for school.

Typically work study jobs don't require too much actual work and sometimes if you're lucky you can study during your work time. I worked in the library for a work study job. When I wasn't checking out books or restocking the shelves I did all my homework and studied, while getting paid! I would challenge everyone who is eligible to try and find a work study position at their school starting freshman year. If you aren't eligible for work study or there aren't many options, try finding a job near campus. You can wait tables, work in a supermarket, landscape, you get the idea. You could also try to find a part time entry level job in your field of study, the options are limitless.

To sum it up, any type of job or income will make you much more comfortable during your school years. Whether it's a work study or just part time work near school, the money flowing in will make your time at school more fun and you might even learn a thing or two on the job. Don't miss out on this cash flow, I highly recommend taking advantage of this opportunity!

Where the heck do you apply for loans?

Okay if you still owe money out of pocket after all of your aid, scholarships, and work study you may need to look into loans. Let's talk about where to find those. I used what's called a Parent Plus Loan from the federal government that was paid directly to my school. You can find the Parent Plus Loan on www.studentaid.gov. When using this loan, technically it's under your parents name, so they are on the hook for paying it back. However, some types of loans can be taken out in your name. There are financial institutions, like local banks and even some credit card companies, that offer student loans as well. This is important: federal loans (like Parent Plus) will have a *lower interest rate* so I would apply for those first before going to any financial institution.

If you want your loans to be in your name, you may need a cosigner (someone on the loan besides you, like your parents) because you likely don't make enough money to prove you'll be able to pay the loan back. The biggest downside of loans is that you need to pay interest on them. Interest begins building once the loans are dispersed (given to the school). There are two different types of loans: subsidized and unsubsidized. The difference is interest, let's check them out.

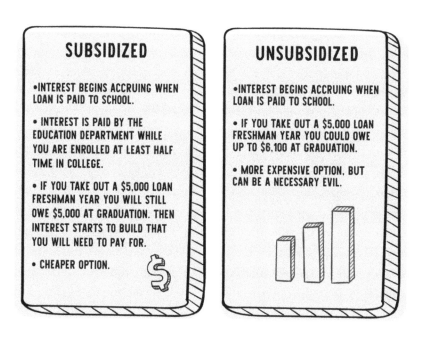

SUBSIDIZED

• INTEREST BEGINS ACCRUING WHEN LOAN IS PAID TO SCHOOL.

• INTEREST IS PAID BY THE EDUCATION DEPARTMENT WHILE YOU ARE ENROLLED AT LEAST HALF TIME IN COLLEGE.

• IF YOU TAKE OUT A $5,000 LOAN FRESHMAN YEAR YOU WILL STILL OWE $5,000 AT GRADUATION. THEN INTEREST STARTS TO BUILD THAT YOU WILL NEED TO PAY FOR.

• CHEAPER OPTION.

UNSUBSIDIZED

• INTEREST BEGINS ACCRUING WHEN LOAN IS PAID TO SCHOOL.

• IF YOU TAKE OUT A $5,000 LOAN FRESHMAN YEAR YOU COULD OWE UP TO $6,100 AT GRADUATION.

• MORE EXPENSIVE OPTION, BUT CAN BE A NECESSARY EVIL.

I know this is a big section, but it's really important and an issue that's not going away. As I am writing this, the total student debt amount is about $1,600,000,000,000.00 or $1.6 trillion dollars. Do a quick Google search and see what it is while you're reading this.

Once school is over, generally loans need to start being paid back six months after you graduate. You get six months called a "grace period" to find a job and get your feet on the ground. I really feel as though high school graduates are not nearly prepared enough to understand loans, how they work and other options available. There simply is not nearly enough education on this. All too often students graduate college and get a massive wake up call that *one third* of their paycheck every week is going to student loans... for the next fifteen plus years! You're locked in until they get back every penny you borrowed, plus interest. Take loans if you need them, there is nothing wrong with that. But really understand the impact they will have once school is over.

I want to quickly take you through a more realistic scenario so you can see how much loans will cost you on the back end once you're out of school. Time really makes the difference, as you'll see below.

Say you take out $50,000 worth of unsubsidized loans at 5.3% (Federal Parent Plus Loan Rate) over the course of four years of college. This means you're taking out a $12,500 loan each of your four years. When you graduate after four years you have borrowed a total of $50,000. But due to the interest accruing when you take the loans out, the balance of your loans is really $54,890.83 when you graduate. Almost $5,000 *more* than you borrowed! You then decide to repay the loans over ten years which is pretty standard, and the interest rate stays the same. Your monthly payments for this would be around $590. So you will pay $590 each month for ten years. Once the ten years is up, you will have paid back the $50,000 you borrowed. <u>But you will also have paid around $16,000 in interest!!</u>

So you went from borrowing $50,000 to paying about $66,000. This is because of something called amortization. What this means is even though you are paying off your loans, interest is still accruing on whatever you still owe. They will charge you interest on the amount you owe until they are completely paid back which is how the $50,000 you borrowed turned into about $66,000 in ten years.

If you want to play around with the numbers Google "amortization table for student loans" and fill out your best guess. You'll quickly see the *real* cost of loans. In short what you need to know about paying loans back is that your payment will stay the same each month until they are paid off. While you are paying them off, they are still collecting interest.

I know I've thrown a lot of info your way, lots of numbers and all kinds of crap. In the end, loans are *loans*. Banks and the government want to get paid for you using their money. That's exactly what interest is, and how they become so expensive. If you are in a situation where you can pay back loans while in school, I highly suggest doing it. It's less money you will pay in the long run. The key takeaway from this entire section on loans can be summed up here: If you need loans, that's completely okay. Just remember the longer you take to pay them back, the more you will need to pay.

FERPA

Another document to be on the lookout for is called the FERPA. This is the Family Educational Rights and Privacy Act. It can be found at www.ed.gov (FAFSA can be found here as well). The FERPA does not affect how much aid you are given, and you do not need to sign it if you don't want to. If you do want to sign it, you will only need to sign the FERPA once your entire college career. What the FERPA does is it gives your school permission to talk to your parents/guardians about your school finances. If you do not sign it, the school will not legally be able to discuss your finances with your parents. If you don't sign it, you may be a "middle man" communicating between the school and your parents about your loans and financial aid. If you want to take care of it yourself, then there is no need to sign it. That being said, trying to figure this stuff out yourself is hard, so I signed mine. This way, if you need help from your parents, it's super easy to get them and the college to talk. No run around.

That is a high level look at your financial aid pathway! You may be thinking schools get paid a lot of money, and you're right. Let's take a look inside, and see how they spend it.

You spend an arm and a leg to go to college. So what do they do with all the money?

Curious what your school does with all the money you give them? I sure was! Let's dive into where all of your money goes! Staff costs are one of the larger expenditures of colleges. Obviously there are professors, but don't forget about custodians, food workers, librarians, technical staff, the works department, student support, accountants, marketers, coaches, and more. Universities employ a lot of people!! Another pretty large part of your tuition goes to campus facilities. It's pointless to be using outdated equipment and facilities, you wouldn't be getting the best education. Schools spend a lot of money on keeping facilities up to date and/or constructing new ones. Depending on the university, housing costs can be pretty expensive. The buildings students live in aren't free. The university needs to pay for them, and pay to keep them in working order. They also need to pay for electricity, sewer charges, water, cleaning staff and products, security, heat and air conditioning, for the dorms and all of the other campus buildings! The list goes on.

Some other things universities spend money on include sports teams, maintenance, clubs, travel, food, and more. I'm not saying it's right for college to be as expensive as it is (and it's getting more expensive). Could some expenses be cut to allow for cheaper tuition? You bet. However, this short snapshot shows that universities do have quite a few expenses! So, your money is going somewhere. It could probably be spent more wisely, but there are a lot of moving parts to take care of.

Chapter Five:

LIFE AT COLLEGE

What is "college life" anyways? Whether you're commuting to school or moving to a new place, "college life" will be different than anything you've experienced before. This section could be endless because of the diversity that surrounds each person and how they experience college. It's so different for everyone that what I write about will likely be much different than what you experience. Regardless, I hope my journey can help provide you with some expectation of what is to come. I don't want to make this section too long, because a lot of this you will need to experience yourself. Most importantly, just know it will be different, and keep an open mind. Don't let yourself get hung up on the small things. Keep moving forward, and you'll be right in the middle of your own experience before you know it.

EVERYONE HAS THE SAME 24 HOURS, CHOOSE HOW YOU SPEND YOURS WISELY.

Time management is one of the biggest challenges you will face in your first year. How we spend, optimize, manage, and save time is something we all work to improve through our entire lives. It seems like our list of responsibilities only gets longer and we are stuck with the same old 24 hours. The truth is, there is plenty of time for everything you want to do if you manage your time correctly. Starting your freshman year with time management in mind will not only help you do better in school, but also allow you to have more fun because you won't be stuck doing homework all the time. Be disciplined to get your work done early, actually focus while you're working, and maybe work in the library to boost productivity. Be proactive when it comes to time management, play offence not defense.

On that same note, time for yourself is important. There will be seemingly endless assignments, but don't get discouraged. Try to find some quality time for you each and every day, this will help with pretty much everything. Some entrepreneurs dedicate one, three, or even up to five hours to themselves each day. They use this time to read, workout, think, run, be with family, or just do whatever they feel like that specific day. It keeps them refreshed and able to deal with everything life throws at them. Now I know this book is about college and this section is about life at college. But, the message here is that time for you is important. You should set aside some time that's nonnegotiable everyday to do what YOU want to do. Whatever you choose, some quality "you time" is good for the soul, and I've found it very helpful in my life.

There may be times at school where you find yourself cooped up in a dorm room or in the library stressing over all the assignments you have, which isn't good for anyone. Almost magically, assignments will get done, and everything will work out. Think for a second about someone you know who has gone to college. On the off chance you don't know anyone, think of me. They made it through, so did I, and you will too. You need to take a step back and remember this is your life. College shouldn't be a time to be locked in a jail cell of a dorm room and not have any fun. You will make it though and be able to have fun along the way, no problem. Don't allow it to be all stress and no fun.

This is a good spot to talk about balance. Something we will revisit over and over in this book. When it comes to life at college, I'm not saying let your grades slip because you're busy "living your life" at parties or whatever. Grades are important and the reason you're here. But, if your grades are in order, then take time for you. I don't believe this life is meant to be spent writing papers and studying, even while in college. What might this "you time" look like? Whatever you want! Get outside, go for a walk, draw something, snap some photos, play frisbee, do whatever it is that gets your mind off school and into the moment. (Now, I know netflix is calling your name and you NEED to see what happens in the next episode, go for it, watch it. But, don't watch the next twenty episodes after that too.) There's something about fresh air and sunshine that's good for the soul. In recap, be a little selfish with your time, doing something you love is paramount, and balance is the key.

Perhaps the furthest thing from high school.

From high school to college there is normally a short time gap of what, three or four months? But high school and college could not be further apart. College is nothing like high school, and high school is nothing like college. Let that sink in. I suppose they could share some similarities if you're living at home. Leaving in the morning, going and doing your work, then coming home. But, everything from the class schedules, to the people, the environment, and the work is so different. Depending on the size of your high school, chances are you knew pretty much everyone in your grade, you at least knew their name. Depending on the college you go to, you may know everyone in your major if it's a small group. My undergrad major had around eighty students freshman year, and of those eighty about sixty went on to graduate. But sometimes, if you attend a larger school, you could sit next to someone senior year and have no idea who they are even though you both have been here four whole years in the same major!

Some larger universities with very popular majors can have literally thousands of students in the same program. More often than not you'll know a few people in other grades, especially if you're in clubs or sports.

But there's going to be a ton of people you don't know at school too. Campuses can get a little crazy with people in different majors, graduate students, visitors, faculty and staff, and others. Some campuses, often ones in cities, are open to foot traffic so it can get even busier between students/staff and people just cutting through campus.

Remember in high school where you only needed to walk down a hallway to get to your next class? In college sometimes a five or ten minute walk across campus will be how you get to class. Pro tip: if you have a bike, skateboard, roller blades, or a scooter (yes even a scooter) bring it! These can not only make your commute to class quicker (meaning more sleep), you can also explore a bigger area around campus without needing to walk or take public transportation.

Cliques

High school was cliquey, remember? That popular group, the football team, the band group, your group. Well, college can be this way too. I would say it's less of an identity in college though. Groups tend to mix a little easier in college, everyone realizes you're all working towards the same thing and can help eachother out. Another big difference between high school and college is how much other people judge each other. Simply put, in college no one cares what you do, how you look, who you're with, or anything. I think what happens is a mix of other people not judging, and you not caring if they do. This is some key advice here, most people are so concerned with themselves that they don't have time to worry about whatever you're doing. And if they do, it's likely they are coming from a place of insecurity.

Another piece of advice I will offer to you is along the lines of no one caring about high school anymore. If you were prom king or queen, the varsity quarterback, star cheerleader, valedictorian, swim champion, or anything like that, nobody outside of your immediate friend group will care. You may get ragged on a little for bringing these things up, so I would avoid it. See in high school there's one varsity quarterback. One prom queen. But when you get to college, there's likely multiple valedictorians, prom kings, star cheerleaders, running backs, or whatever you were. I am not saying you aren't special, far from it. You're unique and I'm sure you have impressive accomplishments. I just want you to be prepared and know this isn't high school anymore. Sure, bring up your accomplishments, but I would absolutely not brag about them. You're in a bigger pond now, fish.

Parties are packed with fun and excitement, but remember: Safety first.

Mom and Dad, if you're reading this before giving it to your graduate, feel free to skip this section, we both know your little angel would never, ever, go to a party… Alright, they gone? Okay here we go. First, to be clear, I am not advocating for under-age drinking in any capacity. If you are under-age, I do not condone drinking. With that being said, this is college and being naive won't help you. It's likely alcohol will be around you, maybe sooner than you think. I just want you to be prepared and have some type of foresight about how this could play out, and more importantly, how to be safe. Partying varies widely depending on schools, dorms, friends, etc. At some schools parties are nonexistent, at others partying is part of the whole school culture. Wherever you go, I have some simple advice for you, and don't overlook it.

No matter what, the buddy system goes a long way. If you're going to a party, go with some friends who will have your back and have your best interests in mind. Secondly and more importantly, be smart. If that means forgetting my first advice and ditching the buddy system to be safe, then do it. If a party is unsafe, don't be afraid to leave. But when you leave, get a ride home. All too often students go to a party and end up in a bad situation or something happens and they never come home. During my four years at WIT, we had three students pass away that were at parties. Bottom line, call for help, walk to get help, whatever you need to do.

Your friends and parents won't be mad if you reach out needing help. Isn't it much better to get a late night call from someone needing help than getting notified something unthinkable has happened? If you need help, get help, don't stay somewhere if it doesn't feel right. Listen to your gut, it's usually right. Here's something I heard at school that I hope will stick with you like it did for me, "They never tell you about the 'punch' in the fruit punch." If you're at a party *do not* take anything from someone you don't know. Don't drink the jungle juice or eat that brownie. There's no way to know what's in it, and that's one mistake you don't want to make.

Another important note here: understand what consent is. Parties can be a blast, and usually are. That's what they're made for right? But sometimes things get out of hand and it's important to know what consent really is, especially if alcohol is involved. Flirting doesn't mean yes. Maybe doesn't mean yes. Changing your mind is okay, and needs to be respected. Only yes means yes. Split second decisions can lead to life changing circumstances. Don't let one decision at a party ruin your life. One way to avoid situations like this, never go somewhere alone with anyone you aren't completely comfortable with at a party. I hope you feel the weight and importance of this short paragraph.

Lastly, never, ever, drink and drive (or ride with someone who's been drinking), no matter what. That one decision can ruin or end your life and the lives of others. And, come on who doesn't have the Uber app? Eat that ten bucks and get a ride. Some universities even have a safe ride system that can get you around campus 24/7 for free. Always know how you're getting home before heading out. There's a lot to experience in college, just be safe while you're doing you, and have fun.

Got Greek?

I was never part of a fraternity so I don't have much in the way of experience for this section. But I can give an overview of what fraternities and sororities are, and what they do. It's pretty common for universities to have both frats and sororities, the only major difference being the sex of the members. Greek life, frats, sororities, they're all social organizations. Membership begins in college and can last a lifetime. On campus these organizations typically have a physical house where members live. To get into a frat or sorority there is usually a rushing period and then a pledge. In simplest terms, rushing is a time period when you can visit different houses on campus to see what they're all about. Members will then send out a formal bid for you to become a part of the house if they liked you and think you would fit in, and once you accept you will become a pledge. At this point, you're in.

There are certainly some big pros to getting into Greek life. One large aspect is the type of work they do. The majority take part in some type of altruistic activities, whether it's community service or raising money for worthy causes. These are great resume building blocks. Houses also host parties, and are designed to build networks while in college. The people in your house can likely be resources for the rest of your life.

I will caution you a little about Greek life, there can be hazing. This is where you are required to do embarrassing, humiliating, and even dangerous things in order to be granted membership. Obviously schools are against hazing, but it's difficult for them to monitor so it can still happen. An initiation is one thing, but if your gut is telling you something is wrong or unsafe, it probably is. There can also be alcoholic concerns with Greek life, parties are usually pretty large and quite frequent. I'm sure you see my point here. There is also a fee associated with joining a house, semesterly dues will likely be sent your way. Be sure to think about this cost if you're considering joining. Finally, don't forget about the time commitment. Like all extracurriculars, there will be a time commitment with joining a house participating in the activities they do. Make sure you take all aspects into consideration before joining, and do what works best for you. If Greek life isn't it, there are plenty of other clubs and groups you can join on campus.

Chapter Six:

TEXTBOOKS

Why are they SO expensive? Alright, here we go with textbooks. I. Hate. Textbooks. Simply because I don't see why a physics book needs to cost $400. Oh, and you need like four to six books per semester. I wasn't a math major but that could be $1,600-$2,400 just for your books. Textbook prices vary widely based on your major. My first semester of college I spent $775 on books. It was a total disaster and of the five books I purchased, at least two I didn't even open. Prices can range from $20 to $500 or more, the cost is nothing to joke about. Here's some advice: If you really think you'll like the topic or are interested in the subject, buy the book. Keep it. If not, then <u>rent it</u>. Rent all of them. It's a much cheaper option, just don't forget to send them back. Trust me, I spent an additional $120 on a book I forgot to send back because they were charging my credit card for four months! Another alternative to buying books is to get an online version of the book, you'll still need to pay for it, but it'll be cheaper. Sometimes if you're lucky there will be a free PDF of the book you need online as well, you just need to find them (but be careful downloading things to your computer). On occasion, college libraries have downloadable textbooks on their websites, something to keep in the back of your mind. Sharing the cost between friends is also an option. If you see people regularly in your class, or someone who even has the same schedule as you, split the cost of a rental. Also check out ThriftBooks at www.thriftbooks.com. They have both new and used books and sometimes you can score a textbook for a way better price than you can find elsewhere.

I purchased some text books freshman year, didn't look at them for three years, and tried to sell them. It wasn't worth the time I put in. Let me say, when you buy a book for $150 and three years later the school bookstore will only buy it from you for $6, you realize you should have rented it. You can always find a book later on if you decide it's something you want to have on hand.

Another tip, ask your professor what year and edition of the book you need. Sometimes professors say last year's book will be fine, or any book within the last three years. This will save you huge bucks. Even last year's copy will be a significantly different price. All information, even most pages, will be exactly the same. Some images may be different and there may be an extra page here or there, but they are almost identical except for the price tag.

The internet is perhaps the most important invention of all time.

In addition to cheaper textbooks, there is an endless amount of information available online that can help you. The internet allows you to have nearly all of the information in the world, right in your pocket, at any given time. Beat that, sliced bread. Here are just a few helpful websites that can do everything from calculus to proofreading and much, much more.

You can visit Chegg at www.chegg.com to order or rent textbooks. If you subscribe, which is around $15 per month, you can also get expert answers to textbook questions. Questions that come right out of your textbooks, thousands of them, word for word. Chegg was one site that helped get me through school, not because of the answers, but because of the explanations. Not all professors will help you work through problems. However, on Chegg the problem will be written out step by step and easy to follow, helping you to actually learn the material. Be careful though, some professors hate Chegg and if they see you've taken a Chegg answer word for word, they may lower your grade or discipline you for cheating. Chegg is a reference, do not copy. If you just copy answers, remember that you may get away with it now, but it won't help you during the exam.

Another amazing (and free) site is Wolfram Alpha at www.wolframalpha.com. This is similar to a Google style search engine. The kicker is you can type calculus problems directly into the search bar and it will calculate the answer for you with a step by step solution. You can also search for anything relating to math, science, technology, art, culture, or everyday life. This is another great site not only for finding the answers, but for being taken step by step through problems so you can figure out how to complete them and see where you're missing steps. If you're a big visual learner then this is a great resource for you.

What if someone could explain the basic steps to you about almost any problem in any subject? Search for Khan Academy on Youtube along with what type of problem you're trying to solve. Whether you're trying to learn Ohm's Law, finance, chemistry, game theory, politics, or coding - there are *thousands* of videos. Each is about ten minutes long and they are incredibly easy to follow. You can also visit www.khanacademy.org, but personally I find just a quick Youtube search to be faster.

Speaking of Youtube, here is another massive resource for finding information about virtually anything. There are how-to videos of *everything* you can imagine. Want more followers on Instagram? Got it. Need to learn how to properly wrap an ankle with athletic tape? It's there. How to design a circuit? Yup. Want to figure out how to be a better marketer? Mhm. I got a ton of tips on how to publish a book from Youtube! You probably know the power of Youtube for some things, but realize how much information is on there. You can absolutely learn the latest TikTok dance on it, but there are also endless videos of each and every subject you will learn about. All for free.

The point of this section is for you to realize the nearly unlimited resource that is the internet. There are no excuses when it comes to finding information because chances are there's a video about it, a website dedicated to it, articles written about it, or something somewhere. Whatever you're having trouble with, you can find it on the internet. These are some great resources to start with. If these can't help with whatever problem you're working on keep searching until you find what you're looking for. I can confidently say I spent as much time looking up questions, definitions, and examples as I did actually doing my work. This sounds comprehensive, but it extremely increased my understanding. You have the resources, use them.

Chapter Seven:

MAJORS, MINORS, & SCHEDULES

> ## " MOST PEOPLE FAIL IN LIFE BECAUSE THEY MAJOR IN MINOR THINGS. "
>
> —TONY ROBBINS

What you pick for a major is a pretty important decision, it will have a profound effect on all types of things we'll get into. And like I said back in the beginning, pick something you're really interested in. With most majors there are a ton of different directions you can go after graduating. Depending on the field you choose you could have nearly unlimited opportunities and you will be qualified to do things you weren't even aware of. The more options the better right?

When picking your major, refer to one of the first sections of this book, where I talk about how you need to do what you love. I'm not sure where you are in your college career when reading this, but it's all the same. Make sure your major is something you really, really love. The reason I say this so much is because I want you to be happy, truly. You deserve to be happy and you should accept nothing less. Think about that and engrave it in your mind. You have <u>one</u> life to live, so why not spend it being happy? If you've picked your major already and think you're going to love it, then dive right in! If you don't end up loving it, let's explore what happens next.

There are some times when people don't exactly know what they've gotten themselves into and have a moment where they go, "Whoa, this is not what I signed up for." If you get to this point, the last thing you need to do is stress. Pause and think: is it just this professor? Is it this specific course? Is it the people I'm with? Is it anything besides the actual major itself? If it is, then those are easy problems to fix. Don't register for a course with that instructor again, accept the fact that some courses will not be your favorite, and you'll learn to deal with all kinds of different people. But, if it's the major itself, if you can't imagine yourself doing what this major will prepare you for, then you may need to make a switch.

This is a lot more common than you'd think. I knew a girl who switched schools AND majors three times in two years. She was going into her junior year of college having majored in three different things, each one at a different school, in three different states! Switching your major is not a huge deal as long as it's early on. I'd say after sophomore year it can get messy, but even then it's not impossible. Sometimes schools accept credits differently and all your credits may not transfer from school to school. That just means you may need to take an extra class here or there, again, not the end of the world. There is also the option to take online classes to catch up or fulfill requirements of the program you want to switch into. If you want to switch to a major that's better suited for you, that you'll enjoy doing and that makes you happy, then go for it. Yes, there may be a bump or two in the road getting there, but it's way easier than it's made to seem. Schools anticipate students changing their majors and have systems in place along with resources dedicated for you to use. You can use your school's resources like your academic advisor for more help. They will help you to understand career options for the program you're in and any others you may want to switch into. Basically, you'll fill out some paperwork and you'll be on your way - no sweat.

Now, if you're like me and get to the end of your degree and find that your major is not what you want to do for a career, there's hope. You have plenty of options we will get to later in the book. But rest assured right now, no matter where you are in the process, you have options.

YOUR WORK IS GOING TO FILL A LARGE PART OF YOUR LIFE, AND THE ONLY WAY TO BE TRULY SATISFIED IS TO DO WHAT YOU BELIEVE IS GREAT WORK. AND THE ONLY WAY TO DO GREAT WORK IS TO LOVE WHAT YOU DO. IF YOU HAVEN'T FOUND IT YET, KEEP LOOKING. DON'T SETTLE.

—STEVE JOBS

Minors can be a major help.

Minors are something that can really compliment your major or help your resume stand out when applying to jobs. Minors usually only require a few additional classes, then you're done. If you're thinking about getting a minor, try to find one that is related to what you want to do in the future. It's pointless to get a minor in something you aren't interested in or want to learn about. It costs money and time, two very valuable things.

Minors can also be a useful way to take classes not normally in your course progression which can give you an edge when looking for a job. For example you could get a chemistry minor to enhance a biology major. There are tons of related combinations you can easily piggy back. There are also an equal amount of combinations not as related, like getting a business minor with a biology degree, and this can also help your resume stick out if you want to do something that mixes those two subjects. Whatever your reasoning for wanting a minor, weigh the benefits and drawbacks carefully. Some schools have a lot of minors to choose from, others only have a few. Do some research on what your school has to offer.

One wall you may run into, is the minor classes won't fit in your major schedule. Your major classes take precedence over minor courses because major courses are required. So sometimes it can be hard to fit the extra classes into an already full schedule. Another problem can be that classes for the minor have prerequisites that aren't included in your major. It's important to look into what is required for the minor before signing up (For example: Algebra 1 is a prerequisite for Algebra 2). So all of a sudden the three extra classes you needed to complete the minor becomes six because of prerequisites, which is a whole semester.

Another difficulty is some minors are only available to certain majors. For instance, some schools don't let engineering majors take a business minor. This can be for a variety of reasons, and whatever the schools claim they are, I disagree with them. However, some schools will make exceptions if you talk to them. All in all, minors can be great if you think they are related to something you want to do in your career or that you're interested in, but they can also bog you down. Do your research before committing to anything.

Set up your course schedule to fit your needs.

What does your ideal college schedule look like? Having all 8 AMs to get your classes out of the way early so you can enjoy the rest of the day? Or starting classes at 2 PM so you can sleep in? Need classes to work around a sports schedule? Or a work schedule? College is great because of the flexibility of the classes. The bigger the school, the more choices you'll have when it comes to a schedule. The big picture is this: say all freshman business majors need to take "Business 101." The school creates course "Business 101" and decides how many sections of the course to schedule. For this example we will assume the Business 101 course meets twice a week. The school could offer four sections of the same class that you get to choose from. They may have different professors, or just meet different times and days of the week, but it's all the same course. For example Business 101 (which meets twice weekly) will have sections as follows:

1) Monday and Wednesday 8-10 AM
2) Monday and Wednesday 12-2 PM
3) Tuesday and Thursday 10 AM-12 PM
4) Tuesday and Thursday 4-6 PM

Those are your choices for Business 101 and you need to pick which section you want to take. Once one section fills up, you need to select a different one. It's important to pick your classes as soon as possible, or you may end up with a schedule you don't like or that doesn't work for you. When picking all of your classes at once, it's like a puzzle. Each class meets at different times and different days of the week, and they all need to fit together somehow. I started using Excel to write out all the courses I needed and tried to make schedules that worked for me. However, there are better resources for you to use. You can go to www.freecollegeschedulemaker. com and build a schedule using their outline. It shows the days and times you'll have classes and even color codes the courses for easy viewing. There are also some apps that can be extremely useful as well. I used "College Schedule Builder" by Kwidil, LLC on the app store. It has a decent amount of colleges listed and, for each school, it has every single class offered for upcoming semesters. You simply select what classes you need and the app will do the work, spitting out all possible variations of the schedule. Then just scroll through your options and pick what you like best. Some semesters you may get lucky and have a four day week, others you may be busy all day, every day. On the next page is one of my schedules when I was a junior at Wentworth. (Yes we had summer semesters.)

SUMMER 2017

	MONDAY	TUESDAY	WEDNESDAY	THURSDAY	FRIDAY
8:00 AM	Medical Devices & Systems	Sociology	Medical Devices & Systems	Sociology	Medical Devices & Systems
8:30 AM	8:00AM -8:50AM	8:00AM -9:50AM	8:00AM -8:50AM	8:00AM -9:50AM	8:00AM -8:50AM
	Annex Central 207	Wentworth 212	Annex Central 207	Wentworth 212	Annex Central 207
9:00 AM	Engineering Mechanics		Engineering Mechanics		Engineering Mechanics
9:30 AM	9:00AM -9:50AM		9:00AM -9:50AM		9:00AM -9:50AM
	Kingman 201		Kingman 201		Kingman 201
10:00 AM					
10:30 AM					
11:00 AM	3D PRINT		3D PRINT		
11:30 AM	11:00AM -12:50PM		11:00AM -12:50PM		
12:00 PM	Wilson 001		Wilson 001		
12:30 PM					
1:00 PM					
1:30 PM			Medical Devices & Systems	Engineering Mechanics	
2:00 PM			1:00PM -2:50PM	1:00PM -2:50PM	
2:30 PM			Ira Allen 125	Dobbs 310	
3:00 PM					

Tuesdays and Thursdays I only had class for two hours which was awesome, 10 AM rolled around and I was done for the day baby. Wednesdays were tough, class from 8 AM until freedom came at 3 PM.

Another tip, do yourself a huge favor and check out www.ratemyprofessors.com before signing up. You'll be able to look up professors at your school and see real reviews from students. Seriously, some professors are terrible and should be avoided at all cost. It will be easy to find the great professors you want to learn from, and avoid the ones you don't. You can visit all of the sites I mention directly on www.tannermcfarland.com/extras anytime.

Last schedule tip, and it's a **game changer**: for the first few days or weeks of class, set your phone background to a screenshot of your class schedule. That way you can reference it conveniently at any time. I'm hoping these tools will make building a schedule easier for you!

Chapter Eight:

COLLEGE MYTHS

Let's dispel come myths, like your major determines your whole life. I'm sure there's a ton of things you've heard about college and among those things some are bound to be myths. I know we have already talked about majors and minors, but I wanted to talk about them again in a different way. First off, a common myth or misconception with college is that your major is your future. Meaning whatever major you pick is what you'll be doing the rest of your life, forever, this is the way it is, no take backsies. Wrong, wrong, wrong. This could not be further from the truth! Your major doesn't need to be your destiny, you can end up doing something completely different. Let's try something, yeah that's right I'm making you actually do something. Ask some adults you know what their college degrees are in, and if you don't already know, ask what they do for a living. Some will match, probably your high school teacher who majored in "Education." But keep looking, you may stumble upon someone like Matt Patricia. He was the defensive coordinator for the New England Patriots from 2012-2017, who got a degree from Rensselaer Polytechnic Institute in Aeronautical Engineering. Wait, what? That's right, he is literally a rocket scientist by trade, but is now a highly successful professional football coach. Mad props. And he's not the only one, there are others whose college majors did not match up to their future as well. Your major doesn't need to be your future if you don't want it to be.

What is the "college experience" anyways?

Ever heard of someone talking about the "college experience" like it's something everyone goes through? Well it's something everyone experiences for sure, but it's also myth number two. The misconception is that the college experience is the same for everyone. It will be significantly different for you than your roommates, your friends, and everyone else. It will be different from my experience too. This whole book is about my experience, and while I hope you can learn from my struggles and advice, the reality is your experience will be your own. People may try to tempt you to do things by saying "You're in college!" or "You're only in college once!" Don't use the excuse of being in college to do something you'll regret. The way you experience college is your own business. Do your own thing and don't worry what other people think of you. If you do that, your college experience will be way more enjoyable than those who try to get the romanticized version from the movies.

Community College < Larger University...? Fake News!

One really frustrating belief surrounding college is that community colleges are of lesser value than "real colleges." Absolutely absurd. If you aren't sure where you want to go and decide to take some Gen Eds at a community college that's great, and you'll save money! If you decide that a community college is the spot for you to complete your degree, kick ass! Just because some schools cost more than others doesn't make them better. Community colleges are almost always the cheaper option and there's nothing wrong with that! Why not get a great education and save a buck (or a few thousand) doing it?

People also talk about your resume after school pertaining to community college vs larger universities or fancy schools. The truth is, the question usually isn't about what school you went to, it's if you can do the job you're seeking. Either way, I believe if you choose to attend a community college or a larger university, you're on equal playing ground. The right school for you is the one you're going to feel most comfortable at. Would you rather have an awesome time at a community college or a terrible time at a "real" university just for popularity points?

Is college even worth it?

There's a myth circulating in the news that, due to the cost, college degrees are becoming no longer "worth it." This may be a question you're asking yourself before going, which is completely justified. In all honesty, college may be worth it, it may not be. This is a really tough one. To start, college is an investment. You invest time and money into it. You will get something out of it - a degree, friends, experience. The thing about investments is that what you get out of them and whether it was "worth it" is different to everyone.

For example, let's talk about money so you can see my point. If you invest $1,000 into the stock market in January and make $100 after one year, was that worth it? Spend $1,000 and have $1,100 after a year. For some people, that's worth it. For others, not worth it. There is no blanket statement about whether money investments or college will be worthwhile to you or not. You need to define what worth means to you. If it means obtaining a degree, hell yeah college will be worth it. If it means finding your life purpose, being top of your class, a high paying job the day after graduation, and an easy rest of your life, well, it may not pan out exactly like that.

College can easily be worth the money and time invested. Some famous college graduates you may know include Warren Buffett, Larry Page, and

Jeff Bezos. Was college worth it to them? It certainly was worth it enough for them to complete their degrees.

On the flip side, some people may not see college this way. I mean, we're talking potentially hundreds of thousands of dollars you need to pay back. Not to mention a couple of years of your life! Some people find this to be too big of an investment for the payoff. Steve Jobs, Bill Gates, and Mark Zuckerberg are three incredibly successful people who dropped out of college. Maybe they found it not useful to spend time and money in school. Look at what they were able to accomplish without a college degree.

Listen, I'm not going to lie to you, college isn't right for everyone. If it's not right for you, don't do it. Plain and simple. It doesn't take college to become successful or rich or happy or fulfilled or any of those things. A degree can be helpful when searching for a particular career, promotion, or job but it's not necessary for everyone. You need to consider what you are putting in, and what you are expecting to get out of college. If they are in line, then you have a good investment. If college won't help you get your ideal outcome from life, maybe it isn't worth it. If it's not, you still have nearly unlimited options. Start a business, go to trade school, apprentice for someone, find a career you like that doesn't require a degree, take a year off to reconsider, use your imagination. Think long and hard about this and do what's right for you.

You won't have any time for anything in college! Wroooong.

You hear it all the time: you won't have any time in college! You're going to be studying 100% of the time. These myths are often told, and usually believed. I would say most people entering college think they're going to be studying an enormous amount. This part of the myth is true. There will be a lot of studying, a lot of working, but that's why you're there, right? It's expected you're going to be working hard. So I'm not going to argue it is going to be hard. However, if someone says you won't have *any* time; that is not true. You will still have time for things like exercise, reading, getting outside, seeing friends, whatever you want.

This is important to me because I have become really conscious of how I spend my time and I think you should too. In everyday life, no matter how old or busy you get, you have time. If things are important to you, you will make time for them. Prioritize your tasks and knock them down. Unimportant tasks can either be delegated to other people, or simply not done. The misconception comes from a mindset of scarcity, there's never enough of anything. But reality is that you have so much more time than you think you do. I was shocked to learn we have 86,400 seconds everyday. Do this right now! Set a timer for fifteen seconds and watch every second go by. Better yet, do a plank on the ground for a measly sixty seconds. You will begin to appreciate how long a single minute is and in doing that, realize how long a 24 hour day actually is. That one minute plank is only 0.07% of your day. Less than one tenth of one percent. Try that same sixty seconds, but instead of planking, scroll through instagram. Time flies by doesnt it?

Think about all the time we spend during the day on our phones and especially on social media. Imagine if you were to spend half as much time on your phone and the time you saved, doing something productive? You would see massive change almost instantly. Some phones have a feature that can show you the amount of time you spend on them, even specifically which apps. Take a look if you can, and think how you could spend half of that time doing something more productive. Check this one out for example. Just half of this time is almost two hours. It's so easy to spend four hours on your phone per day, you may even spend more! So next time you think you don't have time for something, take a look at this bit of data for yourself and then really think if you *actually* don't have time. What could you do with an extra couple of hours per day?

"" TIME IS TRULY THE GREAT EQUALIZER, WE ALL GET THE SAME AMOUNT. ""

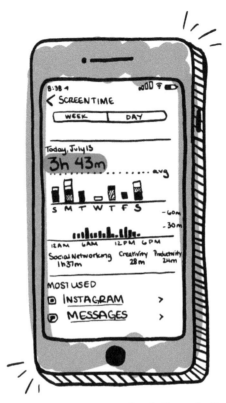

We can't really *save* time, only spend it differently. Be intentional about how you spend your time, especially now. The myth that you won't have time for anything could be true if you let your time waste away on unimportant or inefficient things. But the myth is completely false if you take control of your schedule and use your time wisely.

Can I try your coffee?

Remember when I said time management is one of the most important things you can work on your first year? I want to illustrate time a little better for you if you're still feeling anxious about the time you'll be spending at school. You will have a lot of commitments and work, but really wrapping your head around how long a day actually is will be super helpful. So imagine you go get your iced coffee one morning on your way to class, filled up perfectly to the top. You get to class and right before you go to take the first sip, your best friend wants to try it, so you let them take a sip. You still have the rest of the coffee to yourself, and one little sip isn't that much right? They took maybe... what, like 4% of your coffee? No big deal you hardly notice! It's basically still full even with that 4% missing.

Imagine all the time in a day is like the coffee in the cup. That one sip your friend just took was one hour. One hour is almost exactly 4% of your whole day! It seems like a tiny amount when we're talking about coffee and a huge amount when we're talking about time. But they're really the same thing! If you spend one whole hour doing something, you still have 96% of your day left. Think of what you can accomplish in one hour if you give it laser-like focus. Probably quite a lot! And on top of that you still have 96% of your day left!

It's funny, if I told you to be successful you needed to spend 4% of each day studying you'd probably think that's a piece of cake! But if I say you need to spend an hour each day studying then whoa that sounds like a lot. But they're exactly the same. Once you realize how small an hour is, how small that sip of coffee is, you begin to realize how much you have left. You have the *rest* of your coffee, just like you have the *rest* of your day. Take an hour and study, or work, or exercise, or read. Take just 4% of your day and really focus on what you need to do. You'll have an entire hour to crush your goals, and then you're left with almost your whole day left. Laser focus for one hour, then go finish that coffee and enjoy the other 96% of your day!

Missed my workout today, but the pizza shop cashier's name was Jim so.. Same thing.

Here's a big one… The freshman fifteen! Myth or not? Let's find out. Eating at college is so easy, you get meal swipes or pay for items with your meal plan. This is usually the same for on campus students as well as commuters. Just walk down to the cafe and get whatever you want. Unlimited pizza, fries, pasta, it's all there. The freshman fifteen is (sorta) a myth. This one really depends on you. Your habits are going to determine your weight in college so I would choose what stations you visit in the cafe carefully. In the sense that *everyone* gets the freshman fifteen, that's not true. Some people do, some gain even more, some lose weight, others build fifteen pounds of muscle. It really falls on you.

It's all about the choices you make when going to the cafe, how often you eat out with friends, as well as exercise, fitness level and metabolism. It'll be easy to go overboard and grab three plates worth of food just because you can. Self restraint can be difficult, especially when all that food looks so good! Be sure to think about the consequences of your choices.

A lot of eating at school is about convenience. It's a driving factor in so much of our lives, including food. Take this example: when you get into the cafe isn't it much easier to snag two slices of pepperoni pizza and be outta there than to get in line, construct a salad step by step, and wait for that kid at the dressing station to decide which one he wants for like eight minutes? Like, COME ON MAN JUST USE RANCH. You'd be out of there before you know it with that pizza and your taste buds will thank you. But your body probably won't. Convenience is not always the best idea. Don't get me wrong, pizza is probably one of the best foods on the entire planet. But eating it twice a day, everyday, isn't awesome. It goes good going down, but think of how crappy you'll feel later on with all of that grease in your stomach. Another thing that isn't in your favor is that many dorms don't have kitchens so there isn't much cooking you can do. Be careful what you eat at the cafe, it's too easy to slip up, get home for summer, step on the scale, and be horrified.

Studying can be the freshman fifteen's secret weapon. It's so easy to plow through an entire bag of chips, the family sized box of Cheez-Its, or a 1,000+ calorie pint of Ben & Jerry's while you're going through a lecture or some notes. Sure, munching might ease the pain of studying but all those calories will stick with you. The freshman fifteen can be super sneaky, be careful what you're having while you're studying or just hanging out. Don't let it sneak up on you, the pounds come off way harder than they go on! The classic saying, "You get out of it, what you put into it." holds true for your body, too.

Your ID card is just an ID. Or is it?

Not really a myth, but certainly something you deserve some clarity on. First, don't lose it! If you do, you may need to pay to get another one. Huge hassle, so keep it somewhere safe. Now onto the good part: your ID can carry some serious benefits beyond getting you into your dorm room and buying food on campus. It shows that you are currently a college student. Why is this important you ask? Because college students are broke, sorry to break it to you.

Stores and retailers still want you to come and buy stuff from them, even though you may not have loads of cash! To make it easier on your wallet some stores have a student discount. You may have to ask if they have a discount because oftentimes stores don't advertise it well. So whenever you're eating out, buying clothes, or at the mall, be sure to ask about a student discount! Even online stores can have student discounts. All you need is to prove your enrollment with your ID. To get a list of places with discounts started for you: Amazon Prime Student, Audible, Spotify, Apple Music. A quick Google search will reveal hundreds of businesses that offer discounts. Get in the habit of asking if places offer a student discount, the worst that can happen is they say no. Best case they have a discount and you save some money! I used my Wentworth ID all over Boston, Maine and Washington, D.C. and it saved me all kinds of money. If you're buying stuff anyways, you might as well get a discount!

Chapter Nine:
DINING HALLS

Enter the "all you can eat buffet" of dining hall info. Now I know we talked a little about college food earlier, specifically the dreaded freshman fifteen, but I wanted to devote a whole chapter to dining. Let's dive deeper into the mechanics of how dining halls work. Each and every school's dining halls are different. Different types of food, different set ups, different payment methods, and I'll take you through all of it.

Most importantly, dining halls can be pretty unhealthy if you aren't careful. Why? Well, what is their purpose? To get a large amount of students fed. They aren't a five star restaurant concerned with reviews and if you liked the caviar. They are trying to serve massive amounts of students in a timely manner. So, being the healthiest eatery around is not their main concern. Now, they aren't necessarily unhealthy just because of the food they offer. Confused? Dining halls can be unhealthy because of *you*! Every dining hall has pizza, pasta, chicken fingers, fries, and other greasy items. But they also have a salad station, sandwiches, fruit and veggies, smoothies and more! I totally understand it's going to be way easier to go in and grab some chicken fingers and fries before class than to go through the salad line or make a healthy wrap. But pizza, hot dogs and fries every day for four years? Pretty unhealthy. We talked about this. Try to balance yourself, eat the pizza and fries, but don't forget about the salad station. Make a conscious effort to eat for your health. You'll feel better and can avoid the fear of stepping on the scale back home. Not to mention junk food can cause you all kinds of problems including acne, greasy hair, low energy, and moodiness. Get your diet right from the get go, health = wealth.

Eat your heart out (not really).

How do you pay at dining halls? Well that depends on the school. During my undergrad each semester we would choose our meal plan, A, B, or C. Each of these had a specific dollar amount to them (ie B was $749.00 per semester and was the most common choice). When I would go to the dining hall I would grab what food I wanted and go to a register. Let's say I bought a cup of soup, a banana, and a mountain dew. This came to $7.50, and accordingly, $7.50 would be subtracted from my $749.00. Whoa, hold on. You need to pay $749 bucks at the beginning of the semester just to eat? In this case, and a lot of cases, yes. But! You can add these expenses to student loans if needed, it's easy to wrap them in. Anyways, you continue the cycle of buying items throughout the semester until you run out of money. One side note, if you don't run out of money, sometimes it can carry over to the next semester, but check with your school on this. Sometimes schools will keep your remaining balance. If you're left with $459 at the end of the semester, say goodbye to it because you won't get it back and the school just lined it's pockets with your cash.

Another form of payment in dining halls is you load your ID with "swipes" each semester instead of a dollar amount. They will likely also have different plans, like four swipes/week, ten swipes/week etc. In this scenario you go to the dining hall and the register is at the front before you can get in. You swipe your card, subtracting one swipe from your total, and enter the dining hall. Now, you're free! You can eat as much as you want of whatever you want. Seconds, thirds, it's all up to you, all from that one swipe. One drawback of this method is dining halls who use swipes sometimes require you to eat in the dining hall. This means you are not allowed to bring food with you when you leave. If you need to eat between classes or you prefer to take food back to your room this can be frustrating. Schools where you pay a dollar amount are usually the opposite, you can go wherever you want with your food. Head back to your room to enjoy that burger and side salad while watching the next episode on Netflix.

Now you may be thinking the "swipes" meal plan is better because you can eat as much as you want all for the price of one swipe. Not so fast, there have been tons of studies done that show dining halls with the swipe methodology usually produce less healthy students. You are incentivised to eat as much as you can because you don't want to waste your swipe on something small. You get that side of fries and soda you didn't need because just a sandwich isn't enough to justify using an entire swipe! See how this could impact you? It's completely logical to get as much as you can. If I said you get one swipe a week at a grocery store are you going to just get enough, or are you going to stock up a little? In halls where you pay per item, students are less likely to overeat or feel the stress of needing to get the most out of each meal. Makes sense right? If you can go get a dessert or another slice of zah for free you'd be more likely to go get them, rather than if you have to pay.

Eating at the dining halls will likely get old pretty quick. Freshman year it's difficult to stay away because you usually don't have a kitchen to cook for yourself. By senior year, dining halls are more of a last resort. There will likely be alternative options to dining halls at school for you to try. Depending on the size of your school there may be multiple halls, cafe's, restaurants, and food shops. Wentworth had a small convenience store we could use our meal cards at called the C-Store, it was a life saver. Because we used dollar amounts to pay for things in the cafeteria, the same system was used in the C-Store. You picked out whatever grocery items you wanted and the total was deducted from your plan. A lot of schools have options like the C-Store. Of course, there will be restaurants and other places to go off campus as well. Pay close attention to the payment method your school has and how it could affect your eating. If the cafe gets old, know there are many other options on and around campus.

Food tastes better when you eat with friends.

The dining hall is a great place to meet and connect with people. Throughout college I would offer to grab lunch or dinner at the dining hall with people to get to know them better. Sometimes I would be grabbing something quick between classes and see someone familiar but that I didn't know well. It was a little awkward the first few times, but I got to know so many people by going up to them and asking if I could sit and eat with them until class. They literally never said no, and it was another person I could connect with. The great thing about the dining hall is almost everyone goes there almost every single day. There is a ton of foot traffic, which means there is a huge opportunity for you to meet people there. Who likes to sit alone to eat anyways? Some people enjoy this, and there is nothing wrong with it, but most often people would love someone to eat and chat with. There's no reason that someone can't be you.

Chapter Ten:
ROOMATES & HOUSING

Potential best friends, potential nemeses, potentially both? Now, let's talk about roommates. Nervous? Never shared a room before? Never slept in a twin bed? I was nervous to have roommates, especially people I had never met before. When we moved in I had only briefly talked with them online three days before school. (And I had <u>eleven</u> roommates freshman year!) Depending where you come from and your personality, this could be quite the change for you. I had always shared a room with my older brother until he left for college so I knew sharing a space would not be an issue for me, but it could be a major adjustment for you. It's not as scary as it seems though, chances are your other roommate(s) are feeling exactly how you are.

Let's take a second and think about what concerns you have before moving into school. It's a shared space, everything is 50/50 and there is going to be a lot of compromise. I want you to be prepared for the adjustment of living with someone in such a small space. This is a good point for you to think critically about your own habits or behaviors and how they could cause conflict. Do you stay up super late? Like loud music? With all of this in mind, write down your biggest concerns and any habits you think could cause issues with your roommate. This will prepare you for sharing a space and help you identify potential problems before they arise.

_____

_____

_____

_____

_____

There are a lot of things roommates can argue about, like cleaning common spaces, respecting privacy, shared costs, and getting "cabin fever" being cooped up in your room all the time. These are valid pain points and a lot of people butt heads about them. My junior year I had a roommate who would take almost a week to clean any dishes he made. The sink was disgusting and we actually had to sit down to talk about it. He ended up switching to using a lot of paper products to solve the problem. I'm sure you'll be the clean roommate, but one thing to keep in mind is how you would like to be approached if they had an issue with you. That way, if you have an issue with them, you can talk to them in the same way you'd like to be talked to.

One big complaint I hear relating to college dorms is the bed size. People coming from their double, queen, or even king sized beds at home now having to sleep on this dinky twin bed. Seriously, I'm 5'10" and if I lay on my back and stretch my arms out the edges of the twin bed are at my elbows. Lucky for me, I always had a twin bed growing up so personally there was no difference. Now, a twin bed and sharing a room may not sound great to you. But I assure you there isn't anything to worry about, it's not as bad as you think and ultimately it's not forever.

Don't get me wrong, there are horror stories about roommates, but there are also stories about roommates who became best friends and buy houses next door to each other. If you have the chance to select or choose roommates, it's often advisable to find roommates with similar interests as you. There are different ways schools hold the roommate selection process, but usually you have to find a roommate or group to fill the room you're going to be staying in. For example, if you want a room that fits six people, you must form a group of six students to be able to select the room. Schools will help with this process, but usually using Facebook to find and get to know people is a good start. There will likely be a page on Facebook for your class, for example mine was "Wentworth Class of 2018."

One thing that can be extremely helpful is to room with someone in the same major as you. Then you have the ability to do homework together, study together, and help each other not forget anything. It seemed to me when I was in school that people who roomed with others in the same major had stronger friendships and often did better on assignments. My roommate was mechanical engineering and I was biomedical engineering. We had a few gen-eds together, but that was all, and it worked out great. It's something to think about when deciding who you're going to room with.

One thing to remember if you get stuck with some less than ideal roommates is you may be able to switch after the first semester and you will certainly be able to switch after freshman year. There are a few important factors when looking for a roommate, or at least some things that will need to be agreed upon for your housing to be a success. First up, let's talk about understanding where your roommates come from.

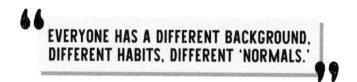

EVERYONE HAS A DIFFERENT BACKGROUND, DIFFERENT HABITS, DIFFERENT 'NORMALS.'

Whether it's your freshman year and you're living on campus, or you've gotten yourself an apartment off campus and are living with a few people, roommates can cause some **serious** headaches. Not to scare you, they can also become your best friends. So, let's hope for the best, and prepare for the worst. Personally I lived with one of the same roommates for all four years of undergrad. Yeah, we had a few misunderstandings and didn't get along 100% of the time, but overall it was a great and comfortable experience. I consider him one of my best friends and we still talk and hang out regularly three plus years after graduating.

My freshman year I lived in a "suite" which was not very sweet. There were twelve of us total. The suite had two doubles, two quads, two bathrooms, and a common room. I can tell you, I am so glad I was in a double and not in a quad. Four guys smushed into a 15'x20" foot space? Can you say no thank you? Coming in freshman year not really knowing anyone and getting into a room with eleven other people was pretty tough. We had some pretty serious issues and one of our mates actually ended up getting kicked out for punching a hole in the wall.

The key to roommates is to understand their background. You need to understand that people are different from you. Some people have no personal boundaries and think it's okay and normal to use your stuff because that's what their background is. You may be the exact opposite and even the thought of someone going through your stuff is stressing you out. That's your background. Your roommate doesnt know that's your background and you don't know theirs, so this could end up being a big issue. Ultimately, transparency is key.

Another aspect that's helpful to know, preferably before moving in, is if your roommate is on a sports team. Athletes in college can have really hectic schedules. Getting up super early for practices and getting back to the room super late after away games. Think about how your schedules will line up. If you're a night owl, but they want to go to bed early it can cause challenges. Again, understand you're different and have different ideas of "normal." This is a good point to talk about how you and your roommate interact.

Be flexible, but have ground rules.

Some ground rules may need to be established up front, but not in a bossy way. Don't be a dictator, try to have a conversation. You may need to tell them "Hey, I really don't like when people go through my stuff so I just wanted to say that up front." Someone else may say "Hey, I don't mind people using my stuff if I can use theirs." You need to see for yourself what your roommates normal is. This is just one example, but there are nearly unlimited things that could cause disputes and one way to avoid almost all of them is to understand that people are different. Learn about your roommates as fast as possible, be kind but clear about your needs, and understand they come from a different background.

Like I said, there will need to be some ground rules put in place to make having roommates an enjoyable experience. One of the key factors is expectations. If you have different expectations then there may be problems. If you're expecting to go to bed at 9 PM but your roommate expects to come back at 2 AM and play some video games, then it's not going to go well. You're going to get mad that they are coming in so late and being loud, and they'll be mad you go to bed so early! Here's a tough pill to swallow: *neither* of you are right! That's right, you are just as wrong as they are! There just needs to be a conversation to solve this. A ground rule like: After 10 PM lights off on weekdays, but weekends can be whenever.

My freshman year I was in a double and my roommate would always play games on his computer super late at night. I would have to get up at 4 AM for rowing practice and sometimes he would still be awake gaming! He woke me up a few times because of noise he made, not intentionally, but this caused there to be a conversation. This isn't like a sit down with your parents. Don't envision that. I mean more like a "Hey dude, you were a little loud last night and it woke me up when you came in. I know I go to bed earlier than you and I don't mind you coming in late, but could you try to be just a little quieter when you come in? I'll be quieter in the mornings too when I get up." (Assuming you get up before them) See? Easy. Who wouldn't be okay with that?

To start a conversation about ground rules, the most important part is to not overthink it. These "rules" are mutual agreements. Things you both buy into so you both can have a better time living together. More often than not it's easy to start a conversation, just come out and say what you need. "Hey I really need to head to bed by like ten, do you think we could have the lights off by then on weeknights?" Rarely will you get a complaint, and if you do, maybe there is a compromise you need to make.

77

You're not going to get everything your way, but you can find a solution that works for both of you.

In my case freshman year, our solution was this: both of our beds were lofted with the desks underneath and we agreed if he was going to come back and play games, he would drape his comforter off the side of his bed to block the light from his computer. This was quieter and the comforter blocked the light so I could sleep through whatever he was playing. I could go on with more stories, but I think you get the point. If there's an issue then you need to talk and come to some sort of agreement that will work for everyone.

PEACE IS NOT THE ABSENCE OF CONFLICT, IT IS THE ABILITY TO HANDLE CONFLICT BY PEACEFUL MEANS.

-RONALD REAGAN

How do you talk to your roommate about something they're doing that's incredibly annoying and they just don't get it? Peaceful confrontation. I would advise you to *not* be passive aggressive because it limits the possible outcomes. And no one likes passive aggressive people, super annoying trait. This will just inflame the situation and significantly reduce the desire to resolve the issue from both sides. I understand there could be some hesitation here. If you find yourself in this situation, what do you do?

First, I would say look at what they're actually doing, take a step back. This may be difficult, but think about what they're doing and how it makes you feel. Does it, PISS YOU OFF? Or, if you were in a better frame of mind, is it just a little annoying? Is it the end of the world? Or, if you take a deep breath, is it just kinda annoying? If you try hard enough to take this step back, I think you'll find that the issue really isn't as big as it seems. If you're reading this thinking "Yeah, yeah whatever. He doesn't get it. They're doing X, Y, Z and man does it piss me off, they do it all the time!" I would ask you, do they *actually* do it all the time? "Yes!" you may be thinking. If the answer truly is yes, then we will get to that. However, if you really try to analyze the situation, it's likely the answer is they don't do it all the time, and when they do it's annoying, but not the end of the world. Taking a step back and cooling off is so important before talking about issues. If you're all shades of pissed off, ready to blow up on them, I'd bet that talk is not going to work out for anyone. You'll end up causing more harm than good and nothing will get resolved. Now that you're in a better frame of mind and not thinking about ripping their head off, let's talk about peaceful confrontation.

One thing that's worked for me is the sandwich approach. Three easy steps which represent the three main layers of a sandwich; the bread, filling and the bread. Step 1: begin with something that you like about your roommate. "Hey thanks for going to lunch with me the other day!" or "I really like your hair today." Something kind that will get *them* in the right frame of mind. Step 2: you can talk about what's getting to you. "Oh yeah, would you mind keeping your laundry on your side of the room?" or "I heard you come in late last night, I know you didn't mean to be loud, but do you think you could try to be just a tad quieter?" Say what you need to to get your message across, but don't be aggressive. Once you've said what your problem is, now it's time to finish the sandwich. Step 3: end with something that's a positive note. That way they will hear your problem, but then immediately get a compliment or something nice right after. Try something like, "Oh I wanted to tell you I have plenty of laundry detergent if you ever need any!" Or whatever works for you. This sandwich can help you in all kinds of situations, so don't be afraid to give it a try in other scenarios too. Try to make it quick, back to back. If you pause and they have time to think, the nice parts of the sandwich will wear off and they will focus on the negative. This approach seriously has worked like a charm for me for years.

Housing is your friend!

Sometimes, unfortunately, roommates just don't click. People can be just too different to have a successful and enjoyable experience. Don't get me wrong, people can be extremely different and still be great roommates. However, if they spread rumors, take your things, use your stuff, are aggressive, or are severely impacting your studies, then maybe things need to change. This is the spot from the previous section I was talking about. The solution to your roommate actually doing whatever "it" is, *all* the time. Enter the Housing Department.

Every school has one and, in my experience, they can be somewhat difficult to deal with but they're helpful. Remember, they think you're important but they also think every other student living on campus is important too. Don't think Housing can control everything, because some things like dorms filling up are out of their control. There is only so much space. If someone is trying to switch out of your room, this could be tough if all other rooms are full. Nonetheless, if you have an issue that you feel you cannot solve, it may be time to go to Housing. Explain what's been happening and either request for yourself to move rooms, or that your roommate switch rooms. If you have multiple roommates, it may be more effective for a few of you to address your concerns to Housing together.

Don't be scared to reach out to Housing. Either email, call, or go in person. Their job is literally to help you, so they will always do their best to solve any problems you have. And if problems get bad enough, they won't let you stay in the room with someone. I hope at this point you're feeling a little more comfortable about roommates. Chances are, it'll work out fine. If things are rough, try the sandwich approach a few times. If that doesn't work, Housing will be able to help. Remember this is all based on my experience and, while I hope my experience helps you, there is a lot of variability with roommates. Who you end up with in a room and how you interact is completely based on who each of you are. The spectrum is wide, you'll come out of it with experience and likely some good stories.

Roommates will probably be a reality of yours for a few years. You may not be sharing an individual room with someone, but it's likely going to be a while until you have your own place. This makes dealing with roommates an essential skill. A lot of people are excited to live in a dorm their first year, living with all your friends like a giant ongoing sleepover. Realistically, that wears off quick and a lot of people want to get out of the dorms as soon as possible. Dorms typically don't have full kitchens, there's a lot of rules and regulations, and there isn't as much privacy as many of us would like. Understandably, a lot of people try to get off campus and find an apartment with some friends, which we'll get to in just a second. First, let's talk about some rules that come with living on campus.

On campus housing is an experience to say the least. Lots of great and entertaining stories come out of living in the dorms. Living on any campus also comes with quite a few rules you'll need to abide by. This is great because it keeps people from being super loud all night, but is also kind of lame because of random room checks, tattle tails, long lists of prohibited items, no privacy and more. This can get old quick. Schools often guarantee on campus housing for freshmen but not for anyone else. There is some housing for upperclassmen but schools often assume upperclassmen will live off campus.

Dorms can be fun because you're so close to other people your age, hopefully your friends, and everyone is in the same boat - working towards a degree. It's something you need to wait and experience to really wrap your mind around. If you choose to stay on campus all four years, the rooms generally get a lot nicer as you get to be an upperclassman. I was on campus all four years and senior year I actually had a full kitchen, living room, and two full bathrooms. The best part was I only had to share with two other roommates. This was incredible compared to freshman year with twelve roommates.

Another important thing to know about dorms is random room checks and prohibited items that I mentioned above. Some schools have a policy where your RA can knock on your door and if you are "home" they are going to come in. If you don't let them in, they have a key. They will look around for prohibited items and if you have any they will likely confiscate them. Depending what it is, you may get a fine, have to go to a mandatory class, or worst case get kicked out of housing. Prohibited items can include: drugs, drug paraphernalia, alcohol, candles, pets, space heaters, water beds, weapons of any kind, air conditioners, some types of plants, E-cigs, vape pens, Juuls, large extension cords, coffee makers that have a heat plate, crockpots, tapestries, additional furniture, flat iron, the list goes on. It's important to check with your school before you get in trouble for bringing something. Some of their prohibited items may be surprising.

Now, off campus housing. You will probably be tempted to move off campus during your time at school. There is a lot more flexibility that comes with living off campus. The list in an apartment lease of prohibited items is likely a lot shorter, but still keep an eye out for it. There are also fewer rules, no RA, possibly closer to your car, and more. Look into the lease if you go this route, there are still rules, you don't own the place and you need to abide by the owner's wishes. Off campus housing can be hit or miss. I have seen college students rent front row beach homes, I've also seen people renting apartments that should be condemned. Don't forget you will likely have a longer commute to class if you live off campus and may need to deal with weather if you're walking/biking. If you don't walk or bike, are you taking public transit? There's a fee for public transit you should work into your budget. Look out for these little fees, they can add up!

If you have a car and want to drive to or park on campus, it's almost certain you'll have to buy a university parking pass. They can get expensive depending on the school. Wentworth, being in Boston, charged students $200 per semester for parking and parking spaces were first come, first serve. If you were late and the lots were full, you'd better hope there is room on the road in a metered spot. UNH, on the other hand, charges students $75 per semester and has a ton of parking available.

One great perk of an apartment is access to a kitchen. If you live on campus and have a kitchen, this part applies to you too. With a kitchen comes the ability to cook. And being able to cook is pretty important. This is an opportunity to cook healthy foods, rather than depending on the dining halls. Take advantage of this and use the opportunity to eat healthy and take care of yourself.

It's a big decision whether to live on campus or move off campus. I chose to live on campus for pretty much one reason. Money. It was easier for me to live on campus because the housing charge was wrapped into my student loans. I didn't have the money to rent an apartment and have hundreds of dollars coming out of my account each month. It was easier for me to pay for housing through a student loan and just pay it back later. I could have taken out a personal loan from a bank and paid the rent for the apartment that way. Maybe the bank loan would have been easier to pay back, but to me that was too much of a hassle. I didn't mind living on campus and it meant I was able to keep more of my money in the short term. I will say, an apartment is likely cheaper in the long run due to the interest on your student loans. How will you know what works best for you? Once you get to school, you will quickly realize the "scene" you fit into and where you like to be. Then it comes down to money and what you're comfortable with. The on campus v. off campus decision will actually be really easy for you, you'll see.

In conclusion, a lot goes into housing. See how living on campus goes your freshman year then you'll be able to see how you like it. Think about the money and if you want the monthly rent, utilities, parking, and other expenses of an apartment or if you want the restrictions but ease of living on campus. Both have their ups and downs, just weigh your options.

Chapter Eleven:
SCHOOL WORK

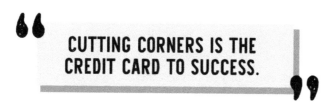

> ## CUTTING CORNERS IS THE CREDIT CARD TO SUCCESS.

This is something a friend of mine once told me. It holds true, everything you put on a credit card needs paying back and with interest. If you cut corners, you will pay in the long run and it will likely be worse than if you had just done the work correctly upfront. You can use a credit card to look rich, but your bank account will be broken. Cut corners and you may look successful, but you really cheated yourself. The workload in college is one of the things complained about the most and it directly relates to this quote. There will be multiple times where you have more than one test, quiz, project and other assignments in the same week. This is not a myth, these weeks really do happen. Did you have midterms or finals in high school? Some people do, others don't. But in college, everyone does. Regardless of major, we all suffer through the midterms and finals together.

Different majors have different types of finals. Big computer programming tests, design critiques, or an exam of everything you've covered since day one are just some examples (yes, that thing you learned on day one that you've forgotten will be on the test). Oftentimes it seems professors can forget that you have other classes, are in clubs or on sports teams, need to eat and sleep and would like at least a sliver of a social life. Overall your personal workload really depends on your school, major, and even what professors you get. I would honestly plan to spend at least five to ten hours per class, per week on homework and studying (one class = five to ten hours total, two classes = ten to twenty hours total etc). The amount of work in college is significantly more than in high school, so be prepared. In the coming paragraphs I'll outline some tips I've learned and experiences I've had to get you thinking about what's to come and how to succeed.

First: Get organized. Then: Stay organized.

Before getting too deep into the workload side of things, let's build a proper foundation together. I've noticed one huge thing about people who are successful in college: they have all their ducks in a row. They're organized! This is not to be understated. Forgetting assignments or losing your homework can really negatively impact you. Everyone has their own style when it comes to being organized, find what yours is and implement it. It's something to work at everyday and something that will absolutely carry over into your professional and personal lives. Too often when class is over kids shove papers into their backpacks to be forgotten until Friday morning when it's time for the assignment to be handed in. Use a binder, colored folders, scan everything to your laptop, or a notebook for every class, but just get organized.

I worked on improving my organization through college and personally saw my grades get better. Not to mention, it feels so much better to get that assignment done the day it's assigned than to forget about it somewhere in your bag until one hour before the deadline. Get some notebooks and label them, keep them in the same spot every day, get a folder or organizer for your papers, and get yourself in a routine to put things where they go. Then, when you need something, you know right where to go. This will be better for your mental health as well, you'll feel a million times better if you're organized. You will be more relaxed, feel more in control, be more confident you're not forgetting anything. It'll also save you time. So, more time for fun things! You get the picture.

Exams and assignments, the meat and potatoes of college.

Okay, now onto the actual work. Assignments and tests are really, really different between majors and professors. Two professors teaching the same course at the same time may provide very different experiences and won't always teach the same material. Weird right? Here's a tip for you: look into your professors before you sign up for classes! I mentioned this earlier, but it's important so I wanted to put it here again. An awesome class schedule, set up exactly how you want it to be will still be miserable if you get professors that are subpar (trust me, some can get pretty bad). You can search professors on www.ratemyprofessors.com to find reviews by actual students. You can also talk with upper class students to hear about their experiences with professors.

For assignments, tests, and other school work, people function differently. If I had a big test I would stay up really late, like 3-4 AM late, the night before to study. That may not be the healthiest way, but that's what worked for me. Other people study a little bit each day the entire week leading up to an exam and that works for them. It's important you find a system you like. The key is finding what works for *you* and sticking to it.

There will be a lot of assignments of all different sizes, kinds, and lengths. Some may take five minutes, others might take fifteen to twenty hours to complete. My best advice is to attack them early, don't wait until the last minute. You don't want to be walking to class trying to scribble down some answers on your way. You'll get a feel for each course pretty quickly, what types of assignments professors give and what they take to complete. One bad assignment won't be the end of things, but do the best you can. If you're having a hard time on an assignment at least give it a try and show you put in some effort. There's no sense in losing stupid points for not turning something in.

As far as exams go, again they can vary quite a bit. I would say most of the time if you fail a test, you will not be permitted to retake it. Sometimes professors have a policy that allows you to retake exams, but it's doubtful. There is no generic or all-encompassing answer for this. For those of you who are self identified "bad test takers" it's going to be even more important for you to study hard. You really need to find a studying system, because one or two courses may have a retake policy, but I would say you won't be so lucky with the rest of your courses. You need to ask yourself how important grades are to you? Even bad test takers can ace exams if they try hard enough. It's work, but it's what you signed up for. Keep your eyes on the prize and keep moving forward.

The only thing the whole group can agree on, is that group projects suck.

I'm sure you've seen memes about group projects. They're hilarious and frighteningly accurate. My favorite one says something to the effect of "I hope my group project mates come to my funeral so they can let me down one more time." It always gives me a laugh. Group projects are almost always difficult. If you get to choose your group, you get with your friends and it can be easy to slack off when you're supposed to be working. If groups are assigned, I mean come on you don't know these people, what if they don't do any work? Or worse, what if they do a lot of work and it sucks? I'm sure you'll run into both scenarios. It's hard getting work done in groups, everyone knows that. You not only need to balance the work, but personalities and schedules clash. Groups need to find a balance and delegate work. One person obviously shouldn't be doing all of the work. Yeah, it's easy to sit back and let Alex do all of the work. He's the smart one anyways, he'll do it right. But what do you get out of that, honestly? Nothing. And if Alex felt like it he could (should) take your name off the project if you don't do any work. The same is true in reverse. It's a dynamic problem, but make sure everyone is doing their fair share.

Here's a tip to get everyone working; delegate tasks which fit people's abilities so everyone has a job. If you're the mathematician but you need a powerpoint presentation, ask Jess to work on getting the presentation set up while you do the math part. That being said, don't make the mistake of forgetting to familiarize yourself with the entire project in case a professor asks you a direct question. Also, address the elephant in the room if someone isn't doing any work. And if simply talking about it doesn't get them in gear, give them something to do and ask them to have it done by a certain time. There's no single solution that will fix all group project tensions, but not doing anything about them isn't going to help anyone either. Working with people is tough, but it's a skill you need because you're going to work with new people your whole life.

Job interviewers often ask about a group project you've done. They may also ask about a confrontation you've had and how you solved it. Some group projects can get pretty hairy and usually professors will understand your concerns if you talk to them about it. But, no matter how bad it is, they're going to ask what you have done to resolve issues. That's a question you should have an answer to (and "I don't know" or "nothing" doesn't count). Group projects are rough, but my best advice is to get them done early and really take ownership of whatever piece of work your name is going on.

One bad assignment won't be the end of you.

Alright, here's the scene: you wake up Thursday morning to your alarm in your dorm room. Before your feet even hit the ground, "SH*T!" You remember you had an assignment due last night and you didn't do it. You didn't even start the damn thing! Panic sets in. You run to your bag or computer to get the assignment. Scramble to get it done without even knowing what the assignment is saying, but you write something down anyway still freaking out.

Hang on a sec.

Take a breath. One late assignment isn't going to kill you. Out of all the assignments you'll do in college if one is late or poorly done, it's not the end of the world. Absolutely don't make a habit of it, but one or two won't be the end of the world. Give yourself a break and get better organized/prepared for the next one.

On that same note, it's just as bad to spend hours obsessing over assignments as it is to lose them. Don't let perfection get in the way of good enough. What that means is don't work something to death trying to get it perfect when it's already *good enough*. This doesn't mean sit back and embrace "C's get degrees" or "What do you call a doctor who got C's? A doctor." Just don't waste all of your time trying to get every last detail exactly perfect. Know when they are good enough to hand in. Otherwise, you'll drive yourself crazy trying to make it perfect.

Imagine if you finish an assignment, then spend three hours doing minor changes. It may only bring your grade from a 97% to a 97.4%. That's not worth it, to me anyways. This is a great example of the Law of Diminishing Returns, shown in the graph below. The more time you spend on a project or assignment, at some point the quality of your work will slow relative to the time you put in. If you keep working on it, at some point, your work may actually get worse because it's over edited!

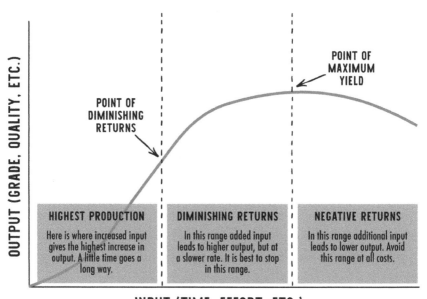

In the end, work on projects until you are comfortable. Remember the Law of Diminishing Returns and don't spend endless hours working yourself to death on a project to only receive an extra 0.1%.

IF YOU'RE GOING TO PROCRASTINATE, PROCRASTINATE BEING LAZY.

Here's a big one, procrastination. The absolute enemy of all college students (and pretty much everyone everywhere, for that matter). Procrastination is the worst thing in the entire world because it's so deceiving. It feels so good to not worry about that project and go to the beach today! Right now! Sun, sand, friends, and the ocean! Or going exploring! Mountaintops, waterfalls and adventures. Who wouldn't love it? Or that pesky "Next episode in 5… 4… 3… 2… 1…" Netflix has now. Yeah, I know, you don't even wait. You rarely see the three because you need to see what happens in the next episode so you click ahead! We've all been there, and it's hard to pull away. However, after your awesome adventures, beach days, and Netflix binges, what happens the night before that presentation or when that paper is due? When you need to review four lectures, make a powerpoint and figure out how to talk in front of your class about a topic you know nothing about besides. This, is procrastination at it's finest.

Assignments only get worse the longer you wait. I know the temptation to start it later. How about we make a deal? Do something, make some type of progress on projects the day they are assigned. I'm not saying finish it, don't look up a hundred sources, but *start it*. Get a rough outline, write something on paper, get your ideas out while it's fresh. This will get the ball rolling and hopefully help you realize it's not as bad as you think. Then you can go on an adventure and have some fun. This way you have a start and it'll be easier to return to.

Moreover, if you get the assignment done early, you can stop worrying about it then go on more adventures, beach trips, and let that Netflix countdown roll all night worry free. You won't feel guilty or harbor any stress from knowing you have unfinished work. Sounds like a good plan, doesn't it? Yeah, but it's hard to *do* it. Hard, but worth it. Remember talking about time management earlier? Be intentional with the time you are spending, and if you put things off until the last minute, it's no one's fault but your own. Honestly, I'm sure you won't listen to this advice right off. But after a couple of nights of being up at 2 AM because your assignment is due in the morning and you haven't even started it, you'll know what I'm talking about. You'll come around.

Well taken notes are worth their weight in gold.

In high school you probably took some decent notes, or at least I hope you did. During class, on films, from textbooks, things like that. Notes in college can honestly make or break you. Yes, they're that important. I'm sure some of you are thinking "Oh, I don't need to take notes, I just remember the important things." I don't suggest just trying to remember everything. You may be able to get away with it for one class, but remembering everything for every class? If you think I'm wrong give it a try through the first exam, but don't say I didn't warn you. If you do decide to take notes, get a seat so you can actually see the board when you get to class. You don't need to sit in the middle of the front row so close you can touch the board, but sitting in the very back row isn't going to help you much. If you can't hear and can't see the board, you're in trouble. Being hidden in the back also creates the temptation to throw in a headphone or go on Facebook, literally anything other than pay attention.

Most professors put lectures online which is cool, you can go back to your dorm and take notes while you're having some nice microwave Ramen and a Gatorade. But be warned, if you think you can doze during the lecture and just copy everything down back in your lair, that's where you're wrong and can get into big trouble.

Most of the time looking at the lectures by yourself later on won't be nearly as helpful as watching the professor go over them, taking notes as they go. Often the slide deck is simple bullet points, and it's what the professor talks about and writes out on the board that's really important. If the professor is going too fast and you can't keep up taking notes, either raise your hand or ask after class if they could slow down. Chances are most of the class is thinking the same thing.

Now, I shouldn't have to say this, but try to write neatly. When you go to review your notes before a test, the last thing you want is to be wondering what your notes say. Taking notes by hand is actually the best way to remember things, even though I know you can type faster. I suggest it, but if the laptop is your thing - go for it!

Power move: if you don't want to write notes, you can also download the powerpoint to your computer and type notes on the corresponding slides. I have seen this work very well for people. Another reason it's great is all the information is in the same place when it's time to study for an exam. Whatever system you choose, get good at it and be consistent.

I'm hesitant to give you this tip. This is one of the best/worst discoveries when it comes to note taking. The best because you can get exactly what you need in a split second. The worst because the chances you will go back and go over the notes is basically zero. Use this as a last ditch effort in an emergency. If you absolutely need to, pull out your phone and snap a picture of the notes on the board (make sure the flash is off or you'll look like an idiot). I took tons of pictures from classes and always planned to go back, but almost never did. Don't use this as your first line of defense, but it can save you if you need.

Not many of you will go to this length, but it will seriously increase what you can retain for knowledge. Buy two notebooks for every class. When you get back to your room at night, copy all of your notes from the day into the other notebook so you have two copies. You'll be surprised how much this will help you.

If that's too much for you, I suggest at least reviewing your notes the day you take them. Just read through what you wrote and make an effort to remember the context and what everything meant. Even this will be a huge help. It will make studying in the future much easier because you have already reviewed on a consistent basis. Why not spend fifteen to thirty minutes each day just reading some notes?

Sounds much better to spend an entire day in the library not understanding what you wrote three months ago right? Can you sense my sarcasm? Okay, keep up with me, onto the next.

Chapter Twelve:
EXTRACURRICULARS

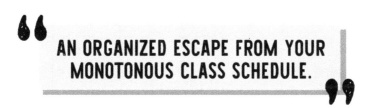

" AN ORGANIZED ESCAPE FROM YOUR MONOTONOUS CLASS SCHEDULE. "

One thing that's important in college is to find people who are interested in the same things you are. Chances are if you have something you're passionate about, there's a club or organization for it on campus. If there's not, it's not hard to start one! Get a small group of people together and find the student engagement center then boom, you have yourself a club.

You can also join a sports team! Whether your college does walk-ons for varsity teams or there are a couple intramural leagues or club sports, go and give it a try. I played soccer year round for many years before going to college. Even though my school had a walk-on opportunity for students, I didn't get the chance to try out. I still wanted to be a part of a team so I did some looking around and it turned out the crew team was holding tryouts! I made the varsity crew (rowing) team at WIT and was in a shell (row boat) for the first time in my life a few weeks later.

HERE'S A PICTURE FOLLOWING MY
FIRST RACE THAT MY DAD TOOK.

MY DAD ALSO TOOK THIS ONE THE SAME DAY, I'M
THANKFUL I GOT TO KNOW THE GUYS IN MY BOAT.

It was awesome to make new friends through that experience, people I never would have met if I didn't go for it. Many of them I still talk to today. The relationships you build from clubs, intramural leagues, varsity sports, or other groups can be some of the strongest in the world. The newness is important as well, some variation in your schedule. Don't just go to class and then go sit in your room all day. The structure of a sport, club, or other organized activity will get you out and about. I highly recommend seeing what your school has to offer and getting involved in something that you'll have fun with.

The great outdoors is, well... great!

It's super important to get outside. This is in the extracurricular chapter because oftentimes it's easy to stay inside if you have no reason to get out. Extracurriculars can be the catalyst that get you some fresh air. And if they really aren't your thing, I'll count regularly getting outside as an extracurricular for you. If going for a walk or chilling on the quad isn't for you, there are still plenty of options. There are all kinds of ways to get involved with clubs, sports, or volunteering that allow you to get out in the sun. I'm going to assume that you enjoy being outside and talk about some things you can do while at school to get some fresh air. You can find a nice place to relax like the quad, by some water, a field, under a tree, or outside a cafe. Wherever you're comfortable, just get outside. People aren't much different than plants; a little fresh air, sun, and water and you'll be doing great. You'll sleep better too, trust me. I know it's much easier to sit idle at your desk, or cuddle in your bed under those fuzzy blankets all day. However, especially during the nice weather months, go for a hike and explore a new area, throw some headphones in and just walk until you feel like turning around. Chances are you'll see something a lot more exciting than what's on your computer or phone screen. If you can't tear yourself away you could even bring your phone or computer outside with you! That's right! Go find a nice bench or bring a blanket to a park and set up shop there! Your body will thank you for getting some fresh air, and you'll find you're much happier too. There has never been a time when I have regretted going outside and being in the sun. My guess is you won't regret getting out either.

I know this chapter was super short, but this is really all you need to know. Extracurriculars are important any way you look at it. Obviously you're at school to learn and be in the classroom, but I believe its vitally important to do things outside of the classroom. In my experience a lot of friendships were made, opportunities found, and experiences were had not in the four walls of a classroom. There isn't a single person I can think of from Wentworth who wasn't involved in something on or off campus. Whether you join a club or organization or find something else, it's all better than just sitting in your door room for four years. For me, one of my biggest regrets from Wentworth was not being more involved. Looking back, there were so many opportunities to connect with people through extracurriculars like sports and clubs that I missed out on. Don't make the same mistake I did, put yourself out there and have some fun.

Chapter Thirteen:

FRESHMAN ⤳ SENIOR YEAR

YOUR YEARLY PLAYBOOK

In this chapter I will do my best to break down each year for you. We'll go over what to expect and what things to keep in mind for each year.

First up, freshman year. This is a time to settle into this crazy ride we call college. No matter if your school is massive or if it's composed of only a couple tiny buildings, freshman year is your time to experiment, explore, and get comfortable. Each year is significantly different, although you may not notice while you're in the middle of it. What I mean is that while you're living it, it will all feel like one big continuation. There will be small differences, but in order to make things easier I want to lay out some big changes and differences you can take advantage of.

Real quick side note. Just like many chapters in this book, I don't want you to believe your experience will be the same exact thing as mine. Chances are yours will be different. This book is not a guide or a process to be followed, but what I learned from college. If you happen to run into similar situations you can avoid all the mistakes I made and take advantage of everything I missed.

Okay, back to it. There's going to be an incredible amount of firsts your freshman year, things you've never done before. It's going to be weird. From roommates, to living on your own, doing your own laundry, feeding yourself, managing your money, no parents to wake you up, no one to force you to do anything, the list could go on. There will be a lot of firsts and this year is the time to take all of them in and to adjust to the newness. Embrace the change and strap yourself in for a hell of a ride over the next few years.

Gen Eds, you'll hate them until you miss them.

What are classes like freshman year? Are they different from high school classes? Great questions. We've already covered workload, but let's talk about what kinds of classes you'll take to start. Freshman year is typically a majority of Gen Eds. Classes everyone needs to take in order to graduate.

Just to give you an idea, let's go over different course plans for a freshman. Each for a different program so we can see a range of required classes. Below there are freshman year courses for an engineering major, a business major, and an education major.

Some typical freshman year courses

	ENGINEERING	BUSINESS MANAGMENT	EDUCATION
FIRST SEMESTER	-INTRO TO ENGINEERING -BIOLOGY -ENGINEERING CALC. I -ENGINEERING PHYSICS I -ENGLISH I	-INTRO TO BUSINESS MANAGEMENT -INFORMATION SYSTEMS -INTRO TO MICROECONOMICS -COLLEGE COMPOSITION (ENGLISH) -GENERAL PSYCHOLOGY	-ENGLISH I -CHILD DEVELOPMENT -INTRO TO PSYCHOLOGY -SEMINAR IN EDUCATION
SECOND SEMESTER	-INTRO TO ENGINEERING II -CHEMISTRY -ENGINEERING CALC. II -COMPUTER CODING -ENGLISH II	-PUBLIC SPEAKING -INTRO TO MACROECONOMICS -MATH PROGRESSION (BASED ON YOUR MATH PROGRESSION IN HIGH SCHOOL) -GENERAL EDUCATION COURSE OF CHOICE -SCIENCE COURSE OF CHOICE	-ART AND SCIENCE OF TEACHING -THREE TO FOUR GENERAL EDUCATION COURSES OF CHOICE OR CONCENTRATION COURSES (FOR A MINOR, IF YOU CHOOSE)

You can see some similarities between these schedules, they all have pretty general classes that other majors could also (and probably do) take. This is great because it makes switching majors relatively easy if you haven't gotten into the super specific courses yet. I encourage you to look up whatever program you like or are interested in, then find the curriculum. It's likely they have an example to show you the exact progression of courses you need to take to graduate and when you need to take them.

Courses that specifically relate to your major won't typically start until sophomore year. Your freshman year classes are non-specific to major and usually not too difficult. But buckle up, because each year classes will get progressively harder. Because most freshmen take similar courses, you'll be in class with students from different majors. This is a great opportunity to get to know some people outside of your major who you may not normally interact with.

You'd think it's probably easier to nap in larger classes right?

Each year your average class size will likely change because your classes become more major oriented, more specific. Your freshman year, when everyone is taking the same Gen Ed courses, your classes will probably be the biggest. As you go through each year they will get smaller and smaller, until it's only the students in your major (which admittedly can still be pretty big). Class size also depends on the school you attend. Some of the larger universities can have class sizes upwards of 1,000 students in a single lecture hall (sometimes an old theater on campus or even a sports arena), while smaller schools can have class sizes of ten or fewer. School and program are the driving factors here. If you go to a large university and enroll in a very popular program, it's likely you will see classes with hundreds of students. If you go to a smaller school, it won't be unusual to have only twenty to fifty students in a course at a time.

Most schools advertise their instructor to student ratio which will allow you to see an average of how many students in each course. For example a ratio of 1:100 would mean on average there is one instructor for every one hundred students. If you think you'll need a lot of one on one time with professors, maybe you need to prioritize a small school or one with a low instructor to student ratio. If you like the idea of a large class in a big lecture hall, move in the direction of a larger school. You'll get a good sense of how it works freshman year, make adjustments accordingly.

 GPA'S ARE WORTHLESS AS A CRITERIA FOR HIRING. WE FOUND THAT THEY DON'T PREDICT ANYTHING.

~LASZLO BOCK

GPA is a tough one, different sides of the same coin really. On one side, you need to take freshman year seriously because it will set the tone for the following years. GPA can be important and if you slack your first year it may be hard to come back from. I've seen it first hand. People who slack freshman year and enjoy all other aspects of college life like partying, Netflix, and sleeping until noon and neglect school itself. When people do this their GPA suffers and they can't recover over the next few years, even with great grades. Sometimes this can even lead to students dropping out. Freshman year was actually my lowest GPA, by a lot. Sometimes I wish I could go back and redo my freshman year, it would have made my overall GPA much better.

Regardless, if this is you, it won't be the end of the world if you do poorly your freshman year. The other side of the coin is that GPA won't make or break you in the real world. My opinion is that you shouldn't be *overly* concerned with GPA. Some employers look at GPA, but I would say most are not too concerned with it. After you have had some experience in the real world, the importance of GPA pretty much goes away. Ask someone you know who went to college and has been working in their field for a few years if their employer looks at their GPA when considering promotions, or if they think it's important if they were to apply for another job. Employers want to know if you are a good leader, if you can be innovative and solve problems, not so much that you failed a biology test because you forgot to study. The reality is, while you're in college it seems like a big deal and it may be to you, but in the grand scheme of life it's not all that important. Do your best to keep it up, you *should* get a high GPA because that's what you're there for, but don't sweat it if you don't have a 4.0 senior year. You will still get a job and you will always have the opportunity to be successful.

> **EVERYONE HAS A PLAN, UNTIL THEY GET PUNCHED IN THE MOUTH.**
>
> —MIKE TYSON

One thing I want to make clear, college is an absolute slap in the face compared to high school. There is much less hand holding, more accountability, and this all comes at once. How hard you tried in high school and how hard you will need to try in college are totally different. For example, I had a pretty easy time in high school. I was top fifty in a class of about two hundred fifty students. This is not me bragging, just setting the scene. I studied for maybe two hours a week and always had really good grades. Mostly A's with a B or two mixed in. During high school I thought I was trying hard. It was hard for me to study for an hour or two a week.

When I got to college, I had to try a lot harder. One to two hours of studying a week was only a drop in the bucket. I thought college was so incredibly hard at first. It was because I was used to trying "hard" by studying a few minutes a day and still getting good grades. Similarly, you may find yourself in a situation where you need to try way harder than you did in high school. Someone who regularly runs marathons once thought a single, measly mile was hard. Make sure you grow and don't get stuck in the past. Change with the changing times.

At some point in your life, you have probably heard someone say "Be proud of what you turn in!" Take that to heart, especially in college. Any assignment you hand in that has your name on it is a direct reflection of who you are. It's very clear if you didn't put in the work and are just handing in a piece of garbage to try and slide by. Don't allow yourself to have standards that low. Anything you hand in, in college and in the working world, you should be proud to have your name on. If you aren't proud, don't hand it in until you are.

Sophomore year, the actual beginning.

By now you have a relative idea of what to expect from your freshman year experience. Lots of new things. New friends, new food, new classes, new professors, new place, new, new new... Sophomore year you will have some familiarity. Going back you'll see familiar places and people, you'll feel comfortable getting around campus. College might not be *home* for you, but you know the landscape. There will be fewer Gen Ed classes and more courses directly related to your major. I'll say it again for clarity: the classes will be directly related to your major. I didn't say they would be related to your career. You'll be in some classes that won't have anything to do in your career.

Take me for example, I am doing nothing even remotely related to Electrical Circuit Analysis and Design. But this was a core class for biomeds. Now, some of my classmates could be using it, but it's not a guarantee. So if you hate a class, you may not need to think about it ever again after the final. That being said, even if classes aren't related to your career, there is a benefit to each class. Whether it's pure information, a new way of thinking, making a relationship, or problem solving. There is a benefit. Some classes you will like, others you will hate. Look forward to the degree and try not to get caught up on one class or one professor you don't like.

Now back to the courses themselves, the core classes you are going to take are likely going to be the foundation for the remainder of your degree. Give these classes some respect, if you slack on these the rest of your degree will be tougher than it needs to be. There's nothing worse than getting to junior or senior year and wasting hours relearning foundational concepts you KNOW were covered in an earlier year. College is like a pyramid, getting more and more focussed or narrow as you climb up. Although more specific than freshman year, the concepts sophomore year are still broad because you're still towards the base of the pyramid.

Is this major or school right for me?

Sophomore year was when I began to realize I didn't love my major. This section could really go anywhere between freshman and senior year, but I'm putting it here because this is when I experienced the feeling of falling out of love with my major. If you find yourself in this situation you can head back to Chapter 7 and look at what switching majors looks like or you can do what I did. I finished my degree even though I didn't love it.

I know, that goes against what I've been saying. But that's exactly *why* I've been saying do what you love. I made some incredible relationships and am glad of the path I took. But looking back, I can't help having a feeling of "What if?" when I think about other paths I could have taken. You can stay with it and see if you start to like it more, or begin to look into other options. Either way, know you aren't the only one feeling this way.

Many acquaintances, few friends.

Sophomore year you may experience a change in your friends. Your freshmen friends may not be right for you anymore. You'll also start meeting tons of new people, the entire incoming freshmen class, new professors, and other people in your building. You'll get to see a lot of new faces. Also quick note, there isn't as much of a stigma around getting to know people older or younger than you in college, like there often is in high school. This makes it easier to meet and connect with more people.

Another tip, older students can sometimes have tips on homework and projects you can tap into. Having a year of college under your belt, you can also spread the love and give some freshmen a few tips. Sophomore year you should pay attention to who you are still friends with, anyone who stuck close to you freshman year could become a lifelong friend. Another note on friends: you don't need to see eachother or speak everyday to still be friends. Like I've said, my college roommate is my best friend but in the past two years I've seen him maybe four times and texted with him only once or twice a month. But everytime I see him, it's like we're right where we left off. These are good friends to keep, remember that.

Free housing hack!

This is the year, if you choose to stay in the dorms, that you can apply to become an RA. There are many perks that come with being an RA, so consider it! You will likely get your housing charge waived and will get a room to yourself. Bonus! So no roommates, and it's free! Sure there are responsibilities that come with the job, but nothing too crazy. You may get a few late calls and disputes to break up, but it's really not a bad job for what it's worth. I wasn't an RA but I wish I was. I had some friends who were and they loved it and thought it was easy! Plus, like I said, they saved thousands of dollars and got a room to themselves.

I think it's important to have the right personality if you're considering becoming an RA. You may have to deal with drunk students, upset students, and other situations you may not be totally trained for. Someone with a strong, confident personality is best fit for this because there is a lot of uncertainty that comes with what kind of calls you'll get as an RA. It's a great opportunity to save yourself some money, just make sure you're up to the job.

Do one thing masterfully, or fifteen things poorly?

Sophomore year is a great time to start refining yourself. It's often better to focus on a few things, than to have a wide range of things you only give a little attention to. I am finding this to be more important as I go through life, focussing on one thing at a time and giving it your best. Sophomore year you can really start putting notable things on your resume. More engagement in clubs, organizations, internships, etc. But don't get caught up in the trap that more is better. It's more important to have a few significant things, than a ton of meaningless bullet points.

While it may be fun and bring variety, hardly anyone remembers the jack-of-all-trades. You don't want to end up a jack-of-all-trades, and a master of none. Decide what things are most important, then begin to focus your time and effort on those things. This will make for a more powerful resume and I believe you'll find more satisfaction as well.

You're the average of the five people you associate most with. <u>Change your circle, change your life.</u>

If you're taking the time and energy required to read this book and actually take in what you're reading, then I give you huge props. I believe you are invested in bettering your future. One way to do that, and you can start anytime, is to build yourself a small circle of powerful people. A team who you think will help pull you in the direction you want to go. If you average out the five to ten people you spend the most time with, you will likely find yourself. You become who you spend time with. Can't you see that? In high school, all the cliques were basically carbon copies of each other. Because they all spent time together and became more like minded. Similarly, you need to surround yourself with people you want to become like minded with. If you ever find that you're the smartest/best/wealthiest person in the room, it's time to find a new room.

Sophomore year is a great time to really focus on who you're spending time with. If you surround yourself with people who are smarter and more organized and more innovative than you, you will learn and become more like them. If you surround yourself with disorganized and lazy people, you will also become disorganized and lazy. Pick who you spend time with carefully.

It may be uncomfortable being around people who you see as "better" than you at something, but understand they are pulling you up and it's to your benefit to do this. If you get put on the fourth string of a basketball team and only hang out with the fourth string players, you will stay there. While there isn't anything wrong with being on the fourth string, if you want to play with the starters you need to practice with them. This goes for all aspects of life, hang with the starters if you want to be one.

Junior year, the sucker punch of undergrad.

Most high school graduates describe junior year as the most difficult year. It was for me, and could have been for you too! Junior year in college will probably be the same. Your classes will likely be most difficult, you're going to need to start thinking about finding a job and where you're going to want to live afterwards. Don't let all of this scare you though. You probably have some time before you get to junior year and there are a ton of resources to help you.

This is also a time to step your game up. When it gets hard, that's the perfect opportunity to really show everyone what you're made of. Most people will get bogged down with the difficulties of the courses, internships, bigger projects, and the thought of being in the "real world" soon. But you need to focus. Focus on what's most important, take a step back, prioritize, and never stop working your ass off. You came to college for a reason, you came here for this. You literally signed up to take these classes, to learn and be challenged, all to benefit yourself in the future. You can either use the difficulties as an excuse to fail and the reason you didn't get where you wanted to go, or you can accept the truth. And the truth is that challenges are opportunities. Opportunities to get better, be better, overcome adversity. It's going to get tough, and when it does, step your game up. See the opportunity. There is no integrity in using challenges as excuses.

A bigger network often leads to a bigger net worth.

I talk about networking in the coming chapters, but I would like to spend a second on it here too. If you're reading this before college, you have some time to prepare! If you're reading this in college it's time to get going! Junior year is often prime time for networking. You are comfortable on campus, know some of the professors, and have an overall sense of what's going on. This is the time to talk to professors about internships, about their experiences, if they can connect you with people in the field that they know. Oftentimes professors can connect you with working professionals in the industry you're trying to get into. This is a great opportunity to pick their brains and get connected with some high power individuals.

I think the best way to approach networking is to start early and just talk with people. Be authentic and be friendly. When you meet people, connect on LinkedIn or via email before the meeting is over. This way you don't just get a business card and forget who they were, or worse, lose their card. If you're ever at a networking event collecting business cards, always try and jot down some notes on their card about them. This will help you put a face to the name later on. Trust me, if you get thirty business cards at an event, you're going to forget almost everyone. People are great resources, so the more people you know, the more resources you have. Get out there, send an email, go to office hours, talk to anyone and everyone and build yourself a powerful network.

A time designed for you to experiment, branch out.

It's quite common to have internships during the course of a degree. Typically they happen junior year, and for my degree we were actually required to have two internships. They were semester long and needed to be full time work (forty hours per week). We were responsible for finding them, the school didn't give that much help. Most Wentworth students got paid for internships because it was full time work for four plus months, but don't bank on all internships being paid, in fact most aren't.

Internships are great opportunities to discover what you like. They are also great opportunities to FAIL. That's right, to fail. If you get an internship and hate it and you think you've failed, good. What if you find an internship and realize this major isn't for you? Good. If you find something you hate, are terrible at, or can't stand, GOOD. You're probably thinking I've lost it at this point, how could getting an internship you hate be a good thing? Because it's just an internship and you've found something you *don't* like to do. Some of the best advice I've received is that internships are important, not so much for finding what you like to do, but figuring out what you don't like to do. It can almost be more helpful to have a bad internship than a good one. You'll find out real quick the things you don't like to do, and can therefore avoid them in future internships or your career search.

I didn't like either one of my internships and they were very different from each other. After, I knew those were two things I did not want to do my whole life. Time wasted? I think not. Better to find something you hate in an internship than in a job after graduation, right? Take whatever comes your way. Experiment, it isn't your career. You may realize you don't like what you thought you would like doing. You may also find that you love doing something you never expected you would like. So take some chances and, at the end of the day, it's a win-win scenario because you will have some type of experience. Either confirming what you like, or exposing what you don't. Internships are awesome, and they will be your first taste of life after college.

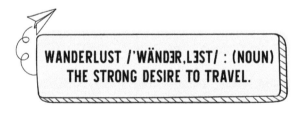

WANDERLUST /ˈWÄNDƏR,LƏST/ : (NOUN)
THE STRONG DESIRE TO TRAVEL.

Junior year is the most popular year to study abroad. Some schools allow studying abroad anytime, but don't count on it. Junior year is really the time to do it. There are pros and cons to studying abroad, and I urge you to look deeper into it than I will go in this book. I never studied abroad so all I can give you is information from the research I've done, people I've talked to who have been abroad, and my own opinion (whatever that's worth to you).

I was actually pretty hard pressed to find someone that didn't like their study abroad experience. In fact, I didn't find anyone who wouldn't recommend it. It seems like if it's something you want to do, chances are you'll like it. Universities have locations all over the world, even smaller schools. Wentworth is a pretty small school and it has the option for students to study in eight different countries at the time of this writing: Ireland, Switzerland, Australia, England, Spain, France, the Netherlands and Germany. Look into what opportunities your school offers as far as locations and time frame. Study abroad programs can range in length from eight weeks long, full semesters, or even a full year. Now let's get you some pros and cons to think about because even though everyone I talked to liked studying abroad, there should always be a lot of consideration before a commitment like this.

PROS	CONS
OUTSIDE YOUR COMFORT ZONE: YOU GROW AS A PERSON WHEN STUDYING ABROAD. A LOT OF PEOPLE'S COMFORT ZONES END AT THE COUNTRY'S BORDERS. DON'T LET YOURS!	**ORGANIZATION:** IT TAKES SOME COURSE BALANCING TO MAKE SURE YOU GET ALL THE BOXES CHECKED TO GRADUATE ON TIME.
INTERNATIONAL NETWORK: KNOWING PEOPLE OUTSIDE THE COUNTRY IS A HUGE LEG UP IN THE WORLD OF NETWORKS.	**MISS TYPICAL COLLEGE:** IF YOU'RE THERE, YOU CAN'T BE HERE. SOME PEOPLE HAVE FOMO ON THE TYPICAL COLLEGE PROGRESSION.
NEW LANGUAGE: YOU WILL LIKELY BE IMMERSED IN A NEW LANGUAGE, TAKE ADVANTAGE OF IT. IT'S A GREAT TIME TO GO ALL IN AND LEARN SOMETHING NEW.	**HOMESICK/LONELINESS:** YOU WILL BE POTENTIALLY THOUSANDS OF MILES FROM HOME, IN A NEW PLACE, AND WON'T KNOW MANY PEOPLE.
NEW LIFESTYLE & CULTURE: IF YOU THINK COLLEGE IS A SHOCK COMING FROM YOUR HOMETOWN, WAIT UNTIL YOU EXPERIENCE A NEW COUNTRY. THROW EVERYTHING YOU KNOW BEHIND AND SEE A NEW PART OF THE WORLD.	**CO$T:** REGULAR COLLEGE IS ALREADY EXPENSIVE ENOUGH. ADD INTERNATIONAL TRAVEL, EXTRA LIVING COSTS, OTHER TRAVEL MONEY, AND FUN MONEY. THE COST CAN SNOWBALL.
NEW STUDY OPTIONS: ABROAD OPPORTUNITIES USUALLY HAVE A MORE DIVERSE CLASS SELECTION FOR YOU TO CHOOSE FROM.	**OVERALL UNFAMILIARITY:** YOU MAY NEED TO TAKE INTO CONSIDERATION EATING AND GREETING CUSTOMS, UNFAMILIAR FOODS, TYPES OF TRANSPORTATION, AND MORE. SOME SEE ADVENTURE, OTHERS SEE PANIC.

I hope this short list gave you at least something to think about when it comes to studying abroad. If you're still on the fence, take a deep dive and do some more research. Your school will have all the resources you need to find out where and when you can go. They may even be able to hook you up with a student who has completed a semester abroad to get their direct experience. If you do end up going, live it up! Before you know it, junior year will have flown by and it'll be time for your final year at college.

Senior year: One chapter ends and another begins.

So, you probably just graduated high school and I'm sure it feels great. You finally made it, congrats! You got over that senioritis you've had since last September. When you get to senior year of college the senioritis will hit even harder. After spending three years in undergrad, you will be more than ready to graduate and turn the page to what comes next. It's going to be really tough to fight through the senioritis, because I'm telling you, it comes on strong. But just as you did in high school, you need to tough it out. Senior year won't always be fun, you'll get stressed and overwhelmed, but that's no reason to stop. You've come this far, why not get a reward for it? This is, again, exactly what you signed up for. Don't let the stress of senior year cause your grades or self care to slip. Enjoy yourself and have fun, but be ready for the fight of your life. Don't get to senior year just to let it all fall apart. Hold it together and rush through that finish line.

There's a lot going on senior year, a lot of moving parts. First I'll take you through the mechanics of the year, what's going on and things you need to do. Then I'm going to talk about applying to jobs and what comes after college. A lot of stuff you worry about freshman year won't matter senior year. You'll know where the buildings are, how the cafeteria works, how to sign up for classes and all that. Senior year is your last year at college and is heavily focussed on your capstone project and planning for life after college.

Capstone Project

Senior year is obviously the last year of college. In order to make it extra fun for you, schools give you what is known as a capstone project. This is one of many things happening senior year that you need to keep a close eye on. The capstone can also be called a senior exhibition, culminating project, or other names. In the end, though, they're all the same thing. A year long project you need to complete and pass to graduate. Your major will determine what kind of capstone you have and the specific requirements you need to meet. For my degree at Wentworth we had to design a new medical device, purchase materials to make it (using our own money), and build some type of working prototype for the final presentation at the end of the year. During my MBA our capstone was to work with a local company to solve a real business problem they were having. We had to present our findings and give our proposed solution on how to best fix their problem.

Capstones are usually done in small groups or individually, no large groups. There's a lot of creativity involved and a lot of the "how-to" of the project is left up to you! I will say they are quite difficult, like they're meant to be, but very rewarding and an excellent resume builder. I can't stress enough how important it is to stay on schedule with your capstone. Don't let yourself fall behind on this! It's very important that you take your capstone seriously. Set yourself a timeline (like a Gantt Chart) and then just chip away at it step by step. Up until this point most projects will be semester long at most. Having such a long time to complete the project almost makes it harder. There is more of a temptation to put it off again and again until you have two weeks left and haven't started. Your group can really make or break the project for you as well. If you have the chance to pick your group, choose wisely! Nothing can ruin a project quicker than a group that can't work together. Sadly, sometimes choosing your friends isn't the best idea, either. Besides your capstone, there are a few other things to think about senior year.

Confirm your degree requirements!

You will want to go over your course catalog and maybe reach out to your student support specialist to make sure you're ready to graduate. Over the four years at school there is a lot that could go wrong without you noticing. You could easily forget a specific elective you needed to take, an internship one summer you forgot to report, or maybe you just need to sign and send in the proper paperwork to graduate. There is a lot you could potentially forget, so early on in the year (maybe even at the end of junior year) make sure you have your ducks in a row to graduate. A few students I knew from Wentworth were not able to graduate on time because they missed an internship or didn't get all the proper documents in order beforehand. You do not want to be that person! Make sure you know what you need to do and get it done early. The sooner the better.

Get your student loans in order.

I know this one sounds thrilling, but it's really important. While your student loans may not be due for a long time when you're reading this, it is a good idea to wrap your head around paying them back. I'm not a fan of surprises, so in my opinion it's better to take a look at them sooner rather than later. This way you know exactly what you're going to owe and when. The smartest thing would be to start paying them off little by little, even if it's just a few spare dollars here or there. Paying even small amounts of loans off before they are due will help you massively in the long run. If you do want to put some money towards your loans, make sure you are paying the principal. Remember, the less you owe (the smaller the principle), the less they have to charge you interest on. Maybe it would be smart to set up a schedule for yourself outlining when to look into your student loans.

Make a list of important dates.

In fact, it would probably be a better idea to make yourself a schedule of *all* the important dates you have for senior year - because there are a lot. You could include when to apply for graduation, you typically need to send in an application and the school will confirm you have met all requirements to graduate. Sounds weird, I know, but it's a thing. You could also include cap and gown pick up, your actual graduation date, parties you want to attend, important capstone deadlines, exams for other courses, or whatever else you think is important! I've found everything goes much smoother when you're organized and have a plan. Don't let life come at you 100mph without any type of plan. Get your schedule in order for senior year and everything will flow smoothly, or smoother I should say.

Your last hoorah!

Going into senior year you might have some type of list, either written down or in your head, of things you wanted to do before leaving college. Senior year is the time to do them! Don't go overboard with anything too crazy, but have fun. Whether it's spending some money at the bookstore to get some school swag before your time is done, pulling an all-nighter, sitting in on a random class (this can be super funny), skipping a class to do something fun, or whatever is on your list. You don't want to look back and think "What if?" One of my greatest fears is becoming old and looking back feeling like I had missed out on opportunities to have fun, make memories, and live in the moment. Someday you'll look back and it's up to you right now to make sure you don't miss out on things. It's senior year, you're going to have a lot of work to do, why not have some fun too? Get yourself a pen and start checking off some of those bucket list items! Alright, now that we've talked a little about the school side of senior year, let's shift our focus to finding you a job.

When should I start applying?

Applying to jobs your senior year will take up quite a bit of your time. It's a long process to search for jobs, tailor your resume and cover letter for each one, and complete applications. There are guides for resumes and cover letters out there (and a couple examples I use on my website at www. tannermcfarland.com/extras), but when it comes down to doing the work and applying, it's a huge time suck. Starting early can be your best friend. Being successful isn't always about being the best, but maybe just getting there first. The early bird may not have the perfect resume, but he still gets the worm. If you apply before everyone else, you may get an interview or offer before others, even if they look better on paper than you.

Don't let excuses get in the way here. It's going to take time, it's probably not going to be fun, but you need to do it! So buckle down, and remember, start early! I'm talking *months* before graduation. Graduate in May or June? Start searching and applying in December. Seriously, the more resumes you have out the better. Keep an eye out for on campus recruiting too! Oftentimes your school will host a job fair where tons of employers will come looking for students to bring their resumes and have a quick chat. If they like your elevator pitch and resume, you may just get a real interview. Job fairs can show you some of the companies in your industry and maybe even help you find a job. That being said, I wouldn't bank on walking out of one with a job. Think of how many students are on campus or in your major, and how many of them the recruiters will talk to. It's certainly worth it to go take a look around, but don't have the misconception that you'll be hired on the spot. Next, let's talk about sending out (a lot of) resumes.

Sounds interesting? Apply, always apply.

What kinds of jobs should you apply for? All of them. Anything that sounds remotely interesting, go for it. The more applications you send means the more options you're likely to have. It's better to have three options and get to choose the best one than to have no options. It's a good problem to have if you get to pick between employers. On the contrary, you're in a really tough spot if you send out one application and never hear back. Depending on your geographic area there will be a range of jobs. Some fields may have thousands of jobs, others may have dozens or less. Searching for different keywords on job websites can give you better results. You may also need to enlarge the geographic area you're looking in, maybe giving yourself a bit longer of a commute. Regardless, apply to any job you think is even slightly interesting.

During my first internship I worked as an additive manufacturing engineer, which is basically a 3D printing engineer. I worked in a lab with a bunch of 3D printers. I can tell you up front I didn't apply because I had always wanted to be an additive manufacturing engineer, for sure not my dream job. However, it was a really cool opportunity and ended up being a pretty awesome internship for what it was. I learned a lot, including like I said earlier,

116

what I didn't want to do for my whole life. The experience I had gained, actually working a full time job and with people in the biomedical industry, was super important. Some of the things I learned and put on my resume became talking points for future interviews. Now this section isn't about internships, but I can give you another example (that I liked better than 3D printing). After graduate school I applied for a position doing CAD drafting because I had pretty significant experience doing it from my time at that internship in the 3D print lab. Was CAD drafting my dream job after college? Nope. But it was interesting enough to apply to and I knew I was capable. Long story short, I got a call, interviewed, got the position, and at the time of this writing I am still working at that company. Turns out it was a pretty awesome job. I had an incredibly flexible schedule which worked well with my work/life balance (I like to work a 6:30 AM to 2:30 PM shift). After a few months as a CAD drafter I was able to get a promotion and now work as a Project Administrator. Still not my dream job, but moving in the right direction. I never would have gotten here without being willing to take the CAD drafting job in the first place! Sure, it's not the perfect job and I know I won't be here forever, but "It checks enough of my boxes!" as my Mom would say.

Here is a little twist to the story that really could have changed where I ended up: I actually almost cancelled the first phone interview because I was so disinterested in just doing CAD, but last minute (literally fifteen minutes before) I decided to take it and it worked out great. Ultimately, apply to anything that sounds even *a little* bit good, it might just turn out to be great.

Another quick tip is to follow up your resume/cover letter with a direct contact. Sometimes it takes a while for anyone to see your resume and sometimes computers weed out candidates based on their resume. First, make sure you tailor your resume and cover letter to use the exact skills and language used in the job description. Second, find a direct contact. Search their website for the HR director or someone from the department you're applying to and directly send them your information, letting them know the position you applied for. This shows initiative and interest. You may not hear back, but it improves the chances that someone (not a computer) will actually review your materials.

Chapter Fourteen:
SELF CARE

Quite cliche but true: What you put in is what you get out. Being alone at college is much different than being at home. At school you're going to need to take care of yourself and eating is a large part of that. I figured this was a good section to hit *after* talking about the freshman fifteen earlier in the book. One of the most basic parts of self care is taking care of your body, you need to fuel yourself with nutritious food and try to live an active lifestyle. I know you've heard this a million times, but if you don't take this seriously you're really going to see the effects in college. The food we put into our bodies affects a large part of our day to day experience. From how we physically feel and sleep, to how we feel about ourselves emotionally. You should eat to fuel your body like a well oiled machine. You wouldn't put dirty, greasy, junk gas in your car and expect it to be running in tip-top shape, would you? So why would you put excess amounts of junk food into your body and expect to feel great? Now, this isn't a diet book, far from it. As you've seen, I'm all about the pizza and everything, but in moderation. It's what you do on a consistent basis that matters. Pizza or your comfort food of choice once in a while isn't bad, obviously, and I encourage you to have it. But if you regularly put processed chemicals and grease into your body, you're going to feel like crap.

Something to think about is that you may be stuck in a cycle of eating poorly, this can be hard to identify because it's what you're used to. Nothing feels wrong, so why should you change anything? Think when your car is due for an oil change, nothing feels different. You've been driving it for a while and if you go another few hundred miles it's probably fine. Then you push it to a thousand miles overdue. Then two thousand miles. Still, nothing feels any different. You keep driving and eventually, one day - complete engine failure. Now you have a totalled car, when just a few days ago you were driving fine! This story is exactly what can happen to you regarding your diet. Maybe you feel fine the way you're eating now, but it could lead to obesity, high blood pressure, or other health complications. Just because you feel fine doesn't mean your diet is in order. Take a hard look at the way you eat. What will my body look like if I have pizza five days a week? Not to mention that weekly twelve pack of soda. Take a look a few years down the road and honestly think about how you will feel. You change your car's oil to make sure it keeps running smoothly for years to come. Why not treat your body the same?

Eating well doesn't need to be a chore either, there are plenty of foods out there that are healthy for you and taste awesome. Take a little time and go find them, there are foods out there to fit everyone's palates. Once you turn the page here in a sec, you might forget what we're talking about here and how important your diet is, but it's the most basic form of self care. Your body is your most valuable asset and if you don't take care of it, it won't take care of you. This body you're in is the only one you get, remember that. I challenge you to refer to this page now and again to remind yourself to eat well. You'll feel better and perform like you want to, physically and mentally.

Energy drinks can help you get the job done, but long term use - no bueno.

Self care is especially important when under stress. Take some time to learn how to limit and deal with your stress in a healthy way. College will put this to the test, so this section is really important. I'm sure you've had some energy drinks in your day, who hasn't? Ever notice what happens after you finish the energy drink, about an hour later? Once your heart rate drops back down and the sugar and caffeine wear off you crash. Often feeling worse than you did at the start. Maybe you go and drink another, then you're really in trouble. Energy drinks are not only horrible for you, they <u>contribute</u> to the problem of being tired. They're a temporary fix. Like putting on a bandaid instead of getting stitches. It might make it better for a little bit, but you aren't solving the real problem. Energy drinks get you going and get you hyped up for a little bit, but then you crash hard. That's not a sustainable way to get anything done. Here's that idea of balance again.

Every now and again go have that energy drink. Crack one open if you think it will give you the final push to get across the finish line. But long story short, they're not a healthy coping strategy. Drinking one, two, three, or more a day can do some serious harm. For those of you out there who love energy drinks, I want you to imagine the side effects of them coupled with the stresses of college. You have a big test tomorrow that you need to study for. Oh and you also have insomnia and your heart is beating out of your chest. Or you have to go give a presentation in front of your class for the first time - stressful right? How about a headache, anxiety and some jittery hands on top of that? You may think they're helping you stay alert and focussed, but they're really just hurting you. Try to wean yourself off of them, drink more water and get fresh air. You can also drink coffee, tea, and other things with lower amounts of caffeine. Still not great for you, but better than energy drinks.

In the end, you don't want to become addicted to them, to the point you're drinking multiple a day. This could lead to becoming caffeine resistant and needing multiple energy drinks to stay awake, pumping 500mg+ of caffeine into your body. Not good. More often than not, cold fresh water will get the job done. If you really need to stay up, get more sleep the night before or manage your time better. Sorry to attack you, but you have more time than you think, a lot more time. Fix the root problem and you won't need to use energy drinks as band aids, effectively forfeiting your health. All in all, try to stay away from energy drinks and other stimulants.

NAP TIME IS MY HAPPY HOUR.

What goes together better than college and sleeping? Go ahead, I'll wait. Alright, there may be a few things better, but it's a good match. Sleeping is awesome and essential to your health, but like a lot of things in this book, it requires balance. Sleep is necessary for humans, if you stay up for multiple days without sleep you will literally go insane, become mentally unstable, have hallucinations, and after more than ten days or so you could potentially die. Okay, that may be extreme, but too little sleep on a regular basis can also cause moodiness, forgetfulness, dizziness, and other side effects. I probably don't need to tell you about the importance of sleep, I'm sure you already can't wait to get into bed tonight. College years are notorious for getting little sleep. There's a lot to do between school work, extracurriculars, and hanging out with friends. For most of you, trying to get more and better sleep is important. For a select few though, college can give ample time for sleeping and, as you'll see, too much can be equally as bad as not getting enough.

I already mentioned the effects of not enough sleep, none of which are good for a college student who is supposed to be learning. On the other hand, if you sleep too much you're at an increased risk for health concerns such as diabetes, heart disease, and stroke. There are other health concerns correlated with sleeping too much as well. If you think you sleep too much or are sleeping more than nine to ten hours a night, I may suggest looking into it. Shoot for the typical seven to eight hours of sleep a night. Some nights when you need to study or be up early, you may only get four hours or less. You might even have an all nighter or two once finals come around.

Some weekends you'll wake up after being in dreamland for twelve hours. Doing either of these extremes a few times is okay but a regular sleep schedule is important, not only to your physical health, but to most aspects of your life. Know what your body needs and go from there. Listening to your body can be one of the most important things you do through college.

For the lucky ones out there who can nap, naps can be a lifesaver throughout college. Unfortunately, I've never been a napping person, I wake up in a worse mood than when I went down. And if you aren't a napping person, you know what I'm talking about. You wake up from an hour nap and you feel like you just got hit by a truck, not knowing what time it is or where you are. Oh and that assignment you said you would do right after this nap? Yeah not happening in my case.

If you are a napping person, you probably think all of the non-nappers are crazy. You can lay your head down for thirty minutes and then you're ready for anything. For you nappers, indulge when you need to. But don't oversleep as discussed before. We already sleep for about one third of our lives, don't sleep your whole life away. If you take an hour nap everyday just because you feel like it and you can, you lose out on 365 hours per year, or about *thirteen extra days of life*. You're in college, get up and create some memories.

Waking up seven minutes before class is not only possible, it's acceptable.

If you live on campus chances are you'll walk, skate, scoot, blade, or once in a while run to class. Depending on how big your campus is, this usually isn't a very long process. Maybe five or ten minutes from your room to your butt in your "unofficial" official seat. Your morning routine can make a world of difference in college. Doesn't a little routine sound nice? Get up feeling good knowing you have time to get ready, find a coffee, and stroll to class with a couple minutes to spare? Setting yourself a morning routine can be some serious self care. It doesn't need to be painful or anything crazy like getting up at 4 AM. But sticking to a routine that gives you enough sleep and enough time to get fully prepared for the day will take an enormous amount of stress off your shoulders. Some people can wake up literally fifteen minutes before class, roll out of bed, change, brush their teeth and make it with time to spare. Whatever routine works for you, get in the habit of sticking to it. Oh, and your classes don't always have to be 8 AMs. Remember, you make your class schedule. Try working it around your sleep schedule so you are at your best for class.

I hope this section doesn't apply to you...

Taking care of yourself includes showering and personal hygiene. I know, it should go without saying, but you and I both know someone who should read this section. In college, when you're always around people, the last thing you want to have is some serious B.O. Shower often, wear deodorant, brush your teeth, that kind of thing. It's even more important when making first impressions. Wouldn't you hate to meet someone important, say for an interview, and all they remember of you is that you were the smelly kid? Don't laugh because a lot of people struggle with this. To make it worse, people usually won't tell you if you are the smelly kid, so take extra precaution. Don't be one of them.

> TAKE CARE OF YOURSELF LIKE YOU'RE SOMEONE YOU LOVE.

Self care is exactly that. Taking care of yourself. This short chapter talked about a few ways you can do that, but ultimately you know what's best for you and what you describe as self care. My definition may be different from yours, which may be different than your roommates or friends. In the end, I believe a healthy body leads to a healthy mind. That means there should be some movement in your life however that suits you. I am also a big believer in people being happy. My definition of happy is likely different than yours. I absolutely cannot binge watch TV for hours a day or sleep past 7 AM without panicking, feeling like my day was wasted. Being what *I* consider productive and waking up at a decent hour makes me happy. Do what makes *you* happy. You wouldn't let someone you love sabotage themselves into being unhealthy and unhappy would you? Then why would you allow yourself to become unhealthy or unhappy? Check in with yourself frequently. Caring for yourself will be extra important these next few years.

Mental Health - Don't struggle in silence.

One important final note in this chapter. Mental health is one of the most serious issues there is surrounding college. It's a lot more common than you think to suffer from anxiety, depression, and other mental health illnesses. Almost 75% of students who suffer from depression do not seek help. And an astonishing 44% of college students have experienced symptoms of depression. Two things are made clear to me from these statistics. First, if you suffer from a mental health issue, *you are not alone.* And second, *you need to talk to someone.* For some reason, there is a stigma around seeking help or talking about mental health. But finding help and talking about how you feel is one of the most important things you can do. There are all kinds of options from staff on campus to local doctors, therapists, counselors, psychologists, and more. Journaling can be incredibly beneficial, but sitting down with someone and digging deeper is unmatched. Oftentimes, especially in college, we can feel isolated and alone. This is not actually the case. You are not unique in the way you feel. Others have gone through what you're going through and have come out healthier, happier, and to live a vibrant life.

You can even talk to your professors! It's not uncommon for professors to change requirements to help students perform better. If you have anxiety or are having trouble in class, reach out to them. They are there to help you. If you are reading this and don't think your mental health is at 100% then it's time to talk to someone. *Talking always helps.* Take it from someone who has felt depressed and anxious before.

At the end of the day, if a friend of yours was having mental health trouble wouldn't you want them to speak up? Obviously you would. Your friends feel the same way about you! Speaking up doesn't need to be uncomfortable or strange! I know plenty of people who see therapists regularly and it's the best part of their week! It's more normal than you would think to go to some type of counselling or therapy. College can be a crazy and emotional time, but you don't need to suffer or go through it alone. If there is one thing you take from this book, I hope this section is it.

National Suicide Prevention Hotline
1-800-273-8255
www.suicidepreventionhotline.org

Substance Abuse and Mental Health Services Administration
1-800-662-4357
www.samhsa.gov

Chapter Fifteen:
FRIENDS

FRIEND REQUEST SENT!

The first days and weeks of freshman year you will meet a lot of people. They may not all stick around though, flash forward to senior year and your friend group will look a lot different. I don't even remember some of the people I talked to at orientation, who they were or what they looked like. If you're wondering where or how to find friends, refer to the clubs and sports section because those are great places to make friends. People with similar interests tend to stick together and clubs/sports are great places to get started. Usually the students you room with will become your friends too, at least for the time being. It'll also be easy to find friends in your classes, especially classes in your major. Just give it some time, everyone is in the same boat. Understand you probably won't find best friends the very first day.

Your school will probably hold some activities the first week of school designed to help you meet people. Wentworth did a "Birthday Buddy" activity where all the incoming freshmen got together and found someone with either the same birthday as you, or closest to it. Then, with your new buddy, you had to play an ice breaker game. Yeah, these can be a little uncomfortable, but after you know someone else's name you'll feel better and can branch out from there.

The rising and falling of friendships.

As mentioned above, accept that friends will come and go throughout school. Some friends from freshman year may resurface later on or they may not. If some drift away for whatever reason, it's not the end of the world. I truly believe the people in your life at any given time are there for a reason, sometimes unbeknownst to you. Ultimately people will come and go and that is beyond your control, but as they come and go, don't let it affect your world because you will always have people around who care. That's what is ultimately important and true in all cases.

Have a tight knit inner circle.

Good friends will stick around and you'll know who they are. Make sure you have eachothers backs. It's better to have a few close friends than to have many meaningless acquaintances. You may seem more popular if you know everyone's names, but you'll be lonely if you don't have any real friends. The real friends may be few and far between, but friendships you develop in college can last a lifetime.

Often the people you knew in high school will drift away and you'll only see them on Facebook or in town on occasion when you're home. Sometimes people from your high school will go to the same school you do. This gives you the opportunity to grow a new friendship with them, or not. Having the shared experience of being from the same town makes for an easy connection. In some instances, maybe they aren't the best people/person and you choose to keep your distance. Use your discretion on this one, but if someone from your high school does go to your school there's the option for a quick and easy friendship. If your group from high school all goes separate ways, it may not be the end of the friendships! I've seen some groups from high school remain close through college even when they go to different schools across the country. Regardless of what scenario applies to you, you will make friends at college. Remember it's better to have a few solid friends rather than a ton of fake friends.

Chapter Sixteen:

MAKING CONNECTIONS

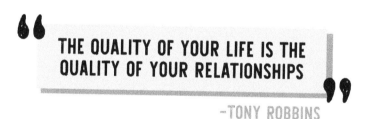

> ❝ THE QUALITY OF YOUR LIFE IS THE QUALITY OF YOUR RELATIONSHIPS ❞
>
> —TONY ROBBINS

Ever heard the saying "It's not what you know, but who you know?" The older I get, the more jobs I apply for, the more people I talk to, this is proving to be true. It isn't always about what you know. You can have the best GPA in your class, be the smartest person in the room, and the most qualified. But unfortunately, sometimes that doesn't matter. Now I want to be clear, I am not saying if you know everyone and have a huge network you don't have to work hard because somebody somewhere will give you a job. That's garbage. You still need to give it your all every step of the way so you can have a strong enough foundation to be successful. What I am saying is the more solid relationships you have the better. That may seem contrary to the last few sentences of the previous chapter, but notice the subtle difference. A ton of fake friends is not going to get you anywhere you want to go. But, a large network filled with strong relationships can really benefit you. Friends and networks are often mashed together into one thing, but in reality they are different. Networks are a group of people that are focussed on business interactions. Friends are people you enjoy spending time with, share mutual trust, and support each other. Sometimes people can belong in both groups, but remember they are certainly different.

When it comes to the people in your network, however big or small it may be, they all know people you don't know. Imagine your network as the image below. It's likely you have a few hundred people in your network. People you know like professors, teachers, coaches, business men and women, your parent's friends, and more. Each of them knows a few hundred more, and on and on.

Sure there's some overlap, but the cycle keeps going. Your network is bigger than you think, you just need to tap into it. Whatever you need, someone in your network can help you get it. As you get older you need to consciously and continuously work on growing your network. This will give you exponentially more opportunities because of the resources your network has. This especially comes in handy when looking for a job. Your network has a much broader reach than you do alone and you should use this to your advantage. Put it out to your network that you're looking for a specific kind of job and let them help you spread the word.

Okay, so a network is great and a bigger network is even better. I know what you're thinking: How do I build a network when I know like eight people? Don't be intimidated or overwhelmed, this is the beginning of something great and it's not as hard as you'd think to build such an incredible tool.

Put yourself out there, see what happens.

There will be tons of networking events to attend throughout school, so dress up business casual and go talk to strangers over a nice cup of water and a couple crackers! Sounds fun, right? If not, you're not alone. But these events could be fantastic and you could meet some amazing people at them. You *should* attend them to try to meet as many people as possible. If you're nervous, go with someone you know and stick together. The fear of standing awkwardly by yourself will disappear if you have someone to fall back on. Beyond little events like this, I have found other ways to expand my network in a more comfortable environment as well. By nature, I am an introvert, always have been. I never liked talking to strangers or putting myself out there. Feel like you're looking into a mirror? That's okay, you're not alone and you *can* succeed at this.

My networking tips start here. Take a moment to remember the last time you saw someone on the street or in the mall do something embarrassing. Even someone you know, like friends, siblings, parents. They tripped and fell, spilled a drink everywhere, or were trailing toilet paper from their shoe. Really take a moment to remember something like this, picture it in your mind. There, you got something? Good. Where is that person now? An hour, a week, month, year later. Probably out laughing somewhere enjoying life, not even thinking about that day. Can you think of the last time YOU were embarrassed? Horrible feeling right? What I am getting at is there have been a million things you've witnessed that have

133

been absolutely humiliating for the person it happened to. That kid trailing toilet paper that you barely remember was so embarrassed when he found out. You forgot about it an hour later. Flip it now, if you were the kid trailing toilet paper, who spilled a drink, whatever. You would be embarrassed, but everyone who saw you forgot within the hour and now **No. One. Cares.** No one cares. No one will remember and if they do, chances are they won't remember it was *you*. It will be "some kid" when they tell the story of what happened.

This is all about getting yourself out there and not being afraid to talk to people. Don't let these excuses and lies you're telling yourself limit you. Pump yourself up. Take control of yourself, your life, your network, and go make it happen. Don't be afraid to embarrass yourself when talking to people because if you do embarrass yourself, first, no one will remember. Second, chances are you won't embarrass yourself, because people want to network with you too. That's the thing, it's a two way relationship. You're trying to grow your network and so are they.

It's actually incredibly easy to talk to most people. There is one sure fire way to get people interested and excited to talk to you. It's a lot simpler than you might think: ask about them. Everyone likes to talk about themselves! Their experiences, feelings, thoughts, and so much more. So ask about them to get started, it's a topic they know *a lot* about so they won't be scarce on information to share. Simply ask an open ended question about them, listen to learn, and ask questions! Make sure you don't ask stale questions though, be genuinely interested. Let me give you a quick example, which of the following questions would you get more excited about to answer?

1. What do you do for work?
2. Based on your journey, what's something you wished you learned earlier?

Sure, it's easier to ask someone the first question and maybe that's the ice breaker. But if you don't follow up with something like number two, the conversation will go nowhere. The second one makes people think and actually engage in conversation, not just give boring answers like their position title, how many years they've been with a company, or where they're from. Seriously, this will work wonders for you. Get out there and get after it!

People don't bite, normally.

Whether you find it easy to walk right up to someone new and introduce yourself, or you're a little more reserved (like me) I have some good news for you. People don't bite. Do not be scared to get out there and meet new people. Growing your network will have unlimited benefits in your future.

Here's a quick story that shows the power of making connections and not being afraid to put yourself out there. When I was sixteen years old I went to take my driving test at the DMV downtown. My Mom drove me and hung out in the lobby area while I nervously sweat to death trying to pass the test (which I did!). While my Mom was waiting for me, she started small talk with a man next to her. His daughter was also there to take a driving test. They got talking about where they each work and the man, we will call him John, worked at Hannafords. A grocery store with scattered locations throughout New England. My Mom told John that it so happened my older brother was looking for a summer job while in college. John suggested my brother come in to talk with him. My brother went in, talked to John, and got a job on the spot. He ended up staying at that job for six years, moving to full time and then up to a management position before moving on to something in his field of study. See how networking can be beneficial? Sometimes even in unexpected ways.

The point is, you never know what a simple "Hey" will lead to. Be nice and respectful to people, you never know what could come of it. People are resources. I don't want this to sound insensitive, because it's not. I'm not objectifying people to be seen as physical resources. But people can provide you with opportunities that can't be found elsewhere. The more people you know and are connected to, the more you can draw from their networks, experiences, ideas, and influences. The more people you know the more resources available to you. This isnt just a taking game, offer your help more often than you ask for help. That is really important. But whether your networking turns into a summer job, internship, career or something even bigger, it's a good idea to get out there and get started.

Chapter Seventeen:
RELATIONSHIPS

College relationships are quite an interesting topic. There is all kinds of advice on what you should do, what not to do, how to get them, long distance, I could go on. Obviously this section will be my opinion, so take it with a grain of salt (like you should all opinions). What you do in college will likely be totally different from my experience, so learn what you can from me but do you.

I'll start by telling you about my relationship with my girlfriend. I began dating her the spring semester of our freshman year and we are still dating (just celebrated our six year anniversary, actually). We dated quite happily through three years of undergrad and then graduate school (an additional one year of school for both of us). Sure, we had some insignif-icant fights and annoyances with each other, but nothing huge. We have a fantastic relationship and did all through college, too.

We went to school about thirty miles from each other and frequently took the train or an Uber to see each other before we were able to have cars at school. It was tough not seeing her during the week, relying on a few weekends a month. But I wouldn't consider this a "long distance" relation-ship. We did make infrequent weekday trips if our class schedules allowed which was great. This is likely what you can expect if you're dating some-one from another school. Some weekend trips, and the occasional weekday hang out if your schools are close enough. Neither of us had other relation-ships in college, so we don't have much in the way of other experience. I will say we made it through because we were focussed on each other. We made time for us a priority and didn't worry about "the college experience" so much. We were happy going through college together, doing our own thing together, and knew that's what really mattered. As long as we were happy, we knew we were doing something right. It's what worked for us and is still working to this day.

College is probably one of the most turbulent times in our lives as far as relationships go. It's not only one of the busiest times of your life with all the classes, new places, and new people all thrown at you at once. It's also a time when people start dating more seriously. You will see a very wide variety of relationships at college. Some people will stay single all through college, others have fifteen partners, some a stable relationship, and everything in between. There is no right or wrong, each of us will go through it differently.

Take a second to understand this next sentence: I believe we know who we are deep down and you simply need to live out your truth. Read it again. If you don't think you're a relationship person right now, follow that path. If you are looking for a relationship, look hard and search wide for the right person. Be yourself and move in a direction that fits who you are. Don't be too rigid with these paths though, something special may come along and surprise you. Don't miss that opportunity. My advice is to be upfront about what you want. Don't go as far as telling them how many kids you want on the first date, but if you're looking for a solid relationship and not some-thing casual that's important to note. No one likes their time wasted, and not being clear about what you want is a great way to waste both of your time. College is a time to have fun and experiment, so again, I say live out who you are and don't apologize for it.

Relationships are one of the most personal things about you. How you interact with and feel about other people is really dependent on your personality, upbringing, and experience. Don't let other people tell you what you can and can't do, or worse, let them alter your beliefs or standards when it comes to relationships. Unfortunately, there is a lot of negativity when it comes to relationships in college. There are people who say long distance doesn't work. But it can. People say if you have a college relationship it won't last. They can (I'm proof!). They'll tell you high school relationships going into college don't last. They can. Or you can't have a serious relationship in college. You can. How about you can't go to college and get married at the same time. You can. See the trend? Some advice that will transcend this chapter and book is that people's opinions are crap. Don't listen to what people think or say, especially about something as personal as your relationships.

There is a big difference between people giving you their opinion and giving you counsel. Opinions can manifest as a reflection of the person giving the opinion. For example, if you tell someone you want to be a millionaire and they give you their opinion that "You can't do that, you aren't smart enough for that." That's a reflection of their own insecurities and shortcomings. They're afraid they can't become a millionaire because they aren't smart enough and can't imagine how that could happen for them. It has much less to do with you and all to do with them. Be weary of opinions. Counsel is given as solid advice for your situation, taking out of the equation the person offering their counsel. People who truly want to see you succeed and who believe in you will give counsel. They will take a hard look at your circumstances and give you advice tailored to you. You want to be a millionaire? They will look at your strengths and weaknesses and help to direct you to success. The same goes for relationships. When people are talking to you, think about if they are giving you advice or counsel. Focus on *your* truth and don't believe everything spoken to you.

You can make any relationship work with the right amount of commitment and work. I have come to know that relationships are work and if you have one, or have been in one, you should know this to be true as well. No matter how similar you are to your significant other, you're different people and it's going to take work to have a successful relationship. If you're willing to put in the time, commitment, and dedication that goes into any type of relationship it *can* work regardless of circumstance.

Here are some quick tips to keep in mind about relationships that I also think are important. Keep expectations realistic. It's college. Between schedules, sports, homework, and everything else that comes up you need to realize it's not going to be perfect all the time. Here is one that needs to be stressed: communication is crucial. There is no successful relationship without lots of communication. Not just about the good, but about the bad as well. Be open and honest if you want it to last. Be flexible. I'm not saying be a "yes man" and cater to their every whim, but compromise on both sides is necessary for success.

Be yourself! It's *so* important to be yourself in a relationship. It's not sustainable (or fun) to pretend you're something you're not. Be authentic, it's the only way to find the right person. Don't pressure or be pressured. I would say go with the flow. You should never feel pressured to do anything in a relationship and you should never put someone in a situation where they feel pressured. Period.

Finally, don't rush into anything. You have time. It's way better to take things a little slower and be comfortable than to get into anything too fast. If you aren't looking for a significant relationship in college, that is okay too. In fact, I would almost argue more people take that path. There is no right or wrong here. You can stay single and just vibe out if that's what you want to do, and maybe it's a good idea to test the waters before jumping into a relationship in college. A relationship is certainly an added element while going to school and some people don't want the added component.

So, relationships, yay or nay? Who knows, don't jump to conclusions! Feel it out as you go and you may get surprised at what you find regardless of what you're expecting. I suggest not setting expectations on yourself and really just living out who you are, that's what's going to make you happiest. College will be full of surprises, which might be half the fun. Embrace it and don't judge others if they choose a different path than you.

Chapter Eighteen:

WORKING ON YOURSELF

 WHATEVER MAKES YOU HAPPY, DO THAT.

College is a time to learn, figure out what you love and want to do, make friends, and have fun. It's a big process and can be a stressful process at times. You need to make sure you find time to work on yourself during the process. What does that mean, work on yourself? It can mean a range of things. You can read books to develop yourself, focus on your love for music, go for walks, or enjoy the outdoors. Whatever gives you joy, you should do that. You need to find what that is for you, work at it, and grow yourself as a person. It seems to me that experiences are worth their weight in gold, so get out and experience some things! Life isn't about how much money you have. Read that again, better yet I'll say it again. Life isn't about how much money you have. It's about being happy, whatever that means for you, and enjoying the time you are here.

Listen, and disappear.

Another way to work on yourself is to listen to music and podcasts. This one hits close to home because I am an absolute junkie for podcasts. I love information about things I am interested in, it's an endless hunger. This is great because I can do something that captivates me while I drive, while I work, while I workout, while I do almost anything really! Now, music could be your fix. If you're into music like I'm into podcasts, then jam out! This is in the working on yourself section, because this is for you. Not only in college, but in life too, you need to work on yourself and your mind. If music clears your headspace and helps you destress, then do it.

Being happy is literally the most important thing in life. I could go on a rant about this, but I won't. Bottom line, listen to some music or some type of media that gets you jazzed, and listen often. It has helped me in so many different ways I had to mention it here for you. It's a way to learn and you should never stop learning. There is something out there content wise for everyone. Find what you like and enjoy, it's almost always free, and you'd be surprised what good it'll do for you.

 MAKE TIME FOR YOUR PERSONAL HAPPINESS.

Working on yourself can come in many ways, shapes, and forms. There is no right or wrong here. It's about you. Do what makes you happy. If it's playing the guitar, play the shit out of that guitar. If it's soccer, get those cleats on and get out on the field. Whatever it may be, it's important. It's been said many times, by many different people, that the key to life is growth. You need to progress. That is where happiness comes from, the journey. So take a step back and see that you and I, your mom and dad, your professor, your middle school crush, and yes - even your suuuper annoying roommate - are all on a journey. We're right in the middle of it, right now. This is extremely important in college because you will be pulled in so many directions. Don't lose sight of the things that give you joy in order to get straight A's or make honor roll. There is more to life than that.

Happiness looks different to different people. What makes you happy may be miserable to other people and vice versa. I urge you to hold back judgement on what makes other people happy. In the end happiness is the goal, and if someone is happy, who are you to judge? Resist the urge to change people who don't conform to your mold of happiness. If your roommate is completely happy playing video games all day and you love the outdoors, don't push the outdoors on them *too* much. They may be totally happy with their video games and that needs to be okay with you. I believe the world needs more happiness, less judgement, and more people being their authentic selves without fear of what other people think of them. It really pains me that people waste even a portion of their lives being unhappy because of what others think, or spend time trying to fit into someone else's mold of what "happiness" is. Work at what you love, continue to develop yourself, I believe this is how you will find lasting happiness. In closing, if you currently feel judged my advice is to judge less. I know it sounds strange, and maybe even backwards. But I've found that when I have stopped judging other people I don't feel as judged. Try and wrap your head around that and think deeply if you're judging others and what would happen if you let that go.

Chapter Nineteen:
RESUME

> ## " THE ONE PAGE SALES PITCH. "

Whether you need to find a job right now or not, pay attention here for when you do. It'll come in handy. So you need to apply to jobs, a lot of jobs. Time to build your resume! Don't let this scare you, don't dread it, don't think it's hard. It's about you and how you want people to view you, this could be fun! Be confident and you will land the right job for you. Your resume is a big part of that, so let's get into how to write one. There's a million different ways to write a resume, how to structure it, where to put information. I will take you through one way to structure it and what I think one should include. Check out this simple outline on the next page.

Name

(222)-222-2222 | youremail@email.com | City, State

Education:

School Name | City, State   Month and year of graduation

Example:

University of New Hampshire | Durham, NH   May 2019

Qualifications:

Software: list softwares you are proficient in

Skills: Communication, Time Management, and other skills you possess

Other categories that fit you better: taylor to your resume

Projects and Research:

Most important project | Class it was for   Date Completed
- Give a few bullets on what you did
- Make sure to include transferable skills, things you learned that you can use at any job
- Ex: Researched and compared pricing on multiple products for quality and cost solution
- Ex: Designed, created, developed, are also good words

Second most important project | Class it was for   Date Completed
- You can also talk about teams you worked on or lead
- This section is meant to be short and sweet
- Convey you have learned skills that are transferable to the position you're applying

Professional Experience

Most recent relevant job/internship | City, State   Date of Employment
- What your position was and your most important relevant responsibility
- Transferable responsibility or qualification
- Worked on a team, individually, or additional crucial tasks to your position

Second most recent relevant job/internship | City, State   Date of Employment
- Ex: Modeled construction plans with precise detail, following municipality requirements
- Ex: Assisted in the development and testing of software for new products
- Ex: Collaborated with internal departments on design functionality and simplicity

Activities/Leadership

Club, Organization, Etc   Date Participated
- How did you demonstrate leadership?
- Did you work for a cause or charity?

Second Club, Organization, Etc.   Date Participated
- Have you been on a sports team while managing school work?
- Done fundraisers, participated in races, or helped at soup kitchens?

Go to www.tannermcfarland.com/extras to download this free template!

I made the header of the resume based on a few I had seen online, but you can choose to design one however you'd like. I thought the idea of having my name right at the top and **bolded** was important so my name stuck out. Then my email, phone number, and location are some of the most pertinent information, this way employers know how to contact me and where I am from.

For sections of the resume I have education first, it was the most recent accomplishment I had or was working towards. I felt putting my alma mater on top would be important so employers know where I went to school and what degree(s) I have. Don't forget to include the city and state of the school, not every person will be familiar with every school. Put the date you completed the degree, if you're not finished you can write "Expected May 2025" or whenever you are scheduled to graduate.

The next section I have is qualifications, which has some subsections in it. Here is where I would list my proficiencies such as Microsoft Office, G Suite (Google trying to sound fancy), Minitab, Solidworks, and other software. You can edit this list as you see fit. I also had a skills subsection where I list other skills like time management, organization, public speaking - things like that.

Projects and research is next. This is a great section to show the employer your best work. Include the date you completed the project, then use three to four bullets to describe what you did. It's important to mention transferable skills, things you've learned in the past that can be applied to this position. If you learned time management, you can apply time management to this position. If you learned to isolate a specific mutated gene of a fruit fly and recorded how it reacts to caffeine exposure, this is a little *too* specific and may not be transferable to what you're applying to. Instead maybe say something like: followed lab standard operating procedures to design and carry out caffeine exposure experiment on fruit flies. You can easily transfer the skill of following operating procedures and designing/ carrying out experiments. You get the point, you want to describe what you did or learned in a way that can be used in the position you're applying for.

Next, the professional experience section is about any internships or jobs you've held. Best case scenario, these are somewhat related to the position you're applying to, but if not that's okay. Again, describe what you

147

did in a way to show you learned skills or expertise that can be used in the position you're applying to. This section is important because most of the questions you'll be asked in an interview will likely be about your professional experience. Be truthful, but show you can relate your experience to the job you're applying for.

Finally, the activities and leadership section. This is somewhere you can really set yourself apart in the resume, so don't skimp on it. I talked about time management, when I rowed crew six days a week while going to school full time. Having to balance nine practices and a meet every week on top of the amount of school work we received was no small task. This section is a great spot to show you're a well rounded person and someone the employer would want to work with. If done correctly, you've shown in the above sections that you are competent to do the job you're applying to. The bad news is, it's likely many other applicants have shown they're competent too. Let your personality show in this section! The employer will more likely hire someone who can do the job and seems fun to work with, rather than just someone who can just complete the tasks of the job.

" WRITE YOUR TICKET TO SUCCESS "

A cover letter is used to supplement your resume and to introduce yourself to your prospective employer. The cover letter is used to draw attention to and supplement your resume. Do not use it to just reiterate your resume; it's a completely separate document and you don't want to hand in the same thing twice. You will need to write a new cover letter for each position you apply for. You can keep the same template and likely a lot of the letter will be very similar, but *do not* submit the same letter to multiple employers. People in the industry talk and if two employers happen to compare your letters and find them the exact same you will become known as someone who cuts corners. Each job is likely different too, so it only makes sense that your cover letters should be different.

As far as writing one, it will be easier to explain everything if I just take you through the guide and explain as we go. Grab yourself a download of this at www.tannermcfarland.com/extras to get yourself started!

Name
(222)-222-2222 | youremail@email.com | City, State

Name
Address
City, State Zip Code

Date

Hiring Manager (or specific person if you know their name)
Company Name
Company Address
Company City, State Zip

Dear Hiring Manager,

Introductory paragraph. This is where you set the hook. Introduce yourself first, who are you, what school you attend, and what your major is. Tell the employer what position you are applying for and where you heard about the job. Quickly describe your interest in the position/company and leave it at that.

Body paragraph. The meat and potatoes. Here you need to show that you understand the position and it's requirements. Then, explain how and why you are the best candidate to fill the roll based on these requirements. Really elaborate on how your personal experience and skills can contribute to the company. Set yourself apart from the other applicants here.

Closing paragraph. Extend your thanks to them for taking their time to look over your materials and consider you as a candidate. Reiterate quickly why you're the best candidate and why you're interested in the position. Why would you be an asset to the company? Tell them what you will do to follow up, outline a call or email later in the week. Close with a final thank you.

Respectfully,
Name signed (insert image of signature like below)
Name printed (typed like below)

Respectfully,

Tanner McFarland

There we go, not too bad, right? There are different formats you can look up, but make sure this document looks clean and organized. Make sure if you use this header, or any other type of format on your resume, that it's the same on the cover letter. You want them to look like they belong together. It's best to address the letter to a specific person, but if you can't find someone then "Hiring Manager" is good too. Make sure it is not longer than one page! If it's more than one page the reader will get tired of reading it and put it down. It's best to be clear, concise, and convincing.

Some more advice around cover letters is to try not to use the word "I" too much, reword your sentences to be more objective. The use of transitional words can help your writing and ideas flow together. Use lots of verbs and action words, this will make you seem action oriented. Also, make sure you proofread before you send, at least twice, and maybe even give it to someone else to review as well. You don't want to find your dream job and send them a letter with a *tpyo* in it.

Talk about this, not that.

We've covered all of the information that you should include while writing a cover letter, but now let's shift gears and talk about what type of information you can choose not to include. Remember, these cover letters are about you. What you put in the cover letter is just as important as what you leave out. I choose to focus on things in the cover letter I would want to talk about during an interview, and leave out things that wouldn't benefit me to talk about. You can be selective about what you include and talk about. Put in the highlights and leave out anything you can't discuss in great detail.

Let me give you an example of what I included and what I excluded. To start, I *included* my senior project. It demonstrated I was able to work on a project over time with other commitments, come up with a novel idea and work to make it reality, work on a team and as an individual, among other things I felt were appropriate for this job as well. I *didn't include* that I was part of WIT's student chapter of the Biomedical Engineering Society. Why? Because honestly we didn't really do much on campus. We had a networking night with some people from around Boston that a few students showed up to, but that was really it. While it may sound good that I was a part of this organization, showing that I was part of extracurriculars, it seemed like I couldn't say much else about it. You have limited space on your resume and cover letter, use the available real estate wisely and with the most impactful things.

LinkedIn, yes, more important than Instagram.

Let's talk about social media, and I'm not talking about Snapchat or Tiktok. LinkedIn is a gold mine of information and resources. You can search for jobs, make connections with people, grow a network; it's like the business version of Facebook, but way better. I highly suggest making a LinkedIn profile as soon as possible. Like today, seriously. Take ten minutes and go make one, right now, then connect with me at www.linkedin.com/in/tanner-mcfarland to start building your network. Then connect with some of your classmates and alumni from your college. Just search for your school and people who graduated will come up. The shared experience of going to the same school will probably get you a connection and an open door for conversation. Employers will often look at your LinkedIn and if you've built it up, they will get a better sense of who you are compared to anything your resume could explain.

As mentioned in the resume section, put the URL of your LinkedIn on your resume somewhere. Also, if qualified, endorse people's skills on LinkedIn. This will make more sense once you have one, but basically you give your word that someone is good at a skill, like management or marketing. The more endorsements you have, the better your profile looks. If you endorse other people they will endorse you back, similar to a "like for like" on other apps. Final piece of LinkedIn advice, I would keep it a professional space. Remember, employers look at this and it should be used to grow a professional network.

Another place employers look? Your other social media pages. They have business and personal Facebook pages, Instagrams, and probably any other social media apps that have come out since writing this. This is probably a good place to note that your social media handle is just as important as what you post. I would caution you not to get too crazy with your handle because companies will certainly find them and if your handle is inappropriate and unprofessional they will take note. Try and keep it simple, I've always kept mine as @tanner_mcfarland so I'm easy to find. When it comes to posting, if you post something and it's out in the world, your employer could (and likely will) see it if they are interested in hiring you. Those edgy posts, twitter fights, facebook battles, insulting comment threads a mile long - they don't go away. Even if you delete them, they're out there somewhere. Be careful what you post and put out to the world, the internet is an elephant and elephants don't forget.

Chapter Twenty :
JOB SEARCH/ GRAD SCHOOL

" BEING EARLY IS ON TIME,
BEING ON TIME IS LATE. "

Searching for a new job, picking a company you want to work for, or canvassing graduate programs may sound like a lot of fun, and sometimes it is, but in the interest of painting you a complete picture, we need to talk about the nuts and bolts of how the process actually works. As far as the job search goes, there are many different approaches we can get into, but there is one thing that holds true: the earlier you apply the better. We already covered this in Chapter 13 when we went over what to expect senior year. I wanted to mention it again because you need to know what to expect once college is done (and it'll go by way faster than you expect). It's so important to have a plan because you don't want to graduate and realize you can't find a job and need to start paying back all of your loans.

Many people go right into the workforce after college. So to say it again, start looking early. You do not want to wait six months after graduation to start applying to positions (Partly because six months is the grace period for your student loans!!!). I don't necessarily have a set in stone piece of advice for the exact time frame, however, employers may take a few days to even look at your resume or materials you submit. Then they need to look at other candidates' materials as well. This could take a few weeks because they aren't only going to consider people who applied the same day you did. Next, applicants are weeded out as they narrow their candidate pool. Finally employers will schedule phone or in person interviews with the remaining candidates. Decision time: the employer will then decide who they liked and get in touch to hire them. As a courtesy, they will probably let other people know they were not selected. The final step is a discussion of the exact employment offer and all the details that go along with it.

If you can't see where I'm going with this, it's that getting hired can be a super long and annoying process! It's best to get resumes out to jobs you like and get them out early. It will be a much better feeling to be early and have a secured position, rather than waiting and having no option but to take anything that comes your way. You don't want your student loans to come due and not have a job to be able to pay them, so get focussed and get on it!

Search high, low, and wide.

When searching for a job there are many options of where to go. It's likely your school has some resources available to help whether it's your academic advisor, a career advisor, or some other position dedicated to helping students find a job once they graduate. They *want* you to find a job. Why? So they can tell future students that 98% of their graduates find jobs. This ultimately helps them get more students interested in coming to their school because they can show a high post-graduate employment statistic.

Besides resources that your school offers, there are numerous websites you can job search on including Indeed, Monster, Google, Glassdoor, and

LinkedIn. They have a ton of parameters which is great because you can get highly specific in your search criteria. Remember, you may need to search hard for jobs you're interested in by using different keywords. I have a biomedical engineering degree but searching for "biomedical engineer" on some sites gave me zero results in my area. That doesn't mean there are no jobs that I am capable of, but I needed to alter my search and keywords. You may have to do this too. Search for other key words or terms similar to your degree and see what's available.

You can also use word of mouth to find a job (this can be where your network from earlier comes in handy). I know a ton of people who got jobs because someone knows someone. Keep your eyes and ears open for opportunities and if one arises, check it out. In the end, you can always turn it down if it's not what you're looking for. You can also look for companies in your field and go directly to their websites for their postings. Some companies only advertise jobs through their own website and do not use other sites like Indeed or Glassdoor, so keep this in mind. It's important to search widely and be determined when looking. There's a job out there, but you may need to sort through two or ten or twenty or fifty or one hundred before you find the right one for you. Don't get discouraged and throw in the towel if you have to apply to a high number of positions, you will find the right one.

Employers will often hire people that "fit" the job, not the most qualified candidate.

Have you ever had a summer job, or a part time gig somewhere? How did you like the employees who worked there with you? Did your boss like them? If you were the boss, would you have hired them? I'm sure there's a range of answers to these questions. I want to focus on the last question though. Would YOU have hired them? Imagine if you were the boss for a day. How would you know who to hire and what criteria to use?

Let's say you're a restaurant manager and you need to hire one of two candidates for a wait staff position. Who would you decide to hire? One has been in the restaurant industry for five years, they were part of the wait staff at a nice restaurant, but isn't pleasant to be around. They don't get along with anyone and are difficult to deal with. The other has only a summer of experience, much less than the first person. However, they're kind and nice to be around, going out of their way to be helpful. Who would you hire? I'm sure some of you, likely a small percent, would pick the veteran worker because of their experience. I bet the majority of people picked the less experienced worker though, and for good reason. Their personality and the fact they are nice to be around is likely the deal maker. Why is all of this important, what point am I making? This is a book about college, how does this fit in?

The point is this: the person you are is just as, if not more, important as your qualifications. If you are a crummy person who is miserable to be around but have an IQ of 180, you're going to have a hard time getting hired and probably even finding friends. Show your passion and show you're interested in the work, ask questions, and that you're engaged. If you do this, I don't think you'll have a hard time finding a job.

Obviously employers take more into consideration than your resume, cover letter, and LinkedIn profile. A lot of weight is put on how you act in person. Being yourself is the most important thing you can do. Whatever that looks like, I will leave to you. I did want to mention again before we move on the importance of your online presence. Someone can put on a good face for an interview, but sometimes it takes checking their social media to see who they really are. It's so important to keep it at least somewhat professional on your socials and with your handles. Employers *don't* want to see your profile @mrrsteelyogirlll6969, try to keep it something a little more tame like @tanner_mcfarland.

Contemplate all the aspects an employer might look at before hiring someone. Now, considering all of them, would you hire yourself for the position you're applying for? Would you *honestly* be a good hire?

Hungry for even more education? Graduate school has you covered.

You're probably reading this early in your college career, so I won't get too ahead of myself. But this is for the curious ones reading. When the time comes to think about the possibility of graduate school there are many things to think about. First, there are often tests you need to take to get in. There is the GRE (Graduate Record Examination), the GMAT (Graduate Management Admission Test), MCAT (Medical College Admission Test), and likely others as well. The GRE is probably most common, it's like the SAT for most graduate programs. The GMAT is geared towards business/finance/management graduate degrees. The MCAT is if you want to become any type of medical doctor or enter the medical field. They are all similar to the SAT for their respective programs or paths, so don't freak out, you just study hard and do your best. Don't worry about them now anyways, you have plenty of time until then. Just something worth noting to prepare for if you decide to take this path in the future. You may be wondering how to search for graduate shcools.

Searching for a graduate school is similar to searching for an undergraduate school. By the time you're ready to start looking for a graduate school, you will likely be pretty confident in what you want to do as a career. Your school will have some resources for you to check out regarding finding schools, so start there. Beyond that, you can use your internet searching skills to find other schools you may be interested in. First, and most importantly for me, was geographic location. I wanted to stay close to home and get out of the city. After four years in Boston, I was ready to have some peace and quiet.

I knew I didn't want to continue down the engineering path and was very interested in business. So I searched around and found the MBA program at UNH. After comparing other programs I selected UNH for a multitude of reasons. The program was only one year long, typically MBA's are two years, it was close to my house, the class size was small, all things that appealed to me. I liked the course progression and what I would be learning about so I took the GRE (twice) and sent in my application.

A huge plus when looking into grad schools, already mentioned earlier, is that you don't always need to get a graduate degree in the same field as your undergraduate degree! This provides massive opportunities to do what you really want and to explore other avenues. If you're considering graduate school, find a school and program that really excites you. One where you will be enthusiastic to learn what is taught, one where you can feel good about what you're doing. It was incredibly exciting for me to take this next step, I hope you find something (whether it's graduate school, a career, or whatever else) that gets you as excited as I was when starting my MBA at UNH.

The application process to graduate school is pretty similar to undergrad. Each school will have a long list of things you need to submit, a checklist of materials you have to provide, etc. One that may be new is letters of recommendation. The number you will need will probably vary school to school, anywhere from one to five letters. I would advise you to get some letters from your favorite professors (or ones that will speak highly of you) but not to *only* get letters from professors. You can ask any employers you have had, coaches, mentors, or anyone you think would give a good representation of you. The school you're applying to will likely send the writers a link to submit the letter of recommendation. So, sorry you do not get to read them unless the professor sends it to you, which is pretty rare. It's less work for you though, you don't have to worry about getting their letter and submitting it yourself. It's also a good idea to keep a portfolio of work you've completed. Sometimes schools will ask to see some projects you've completed and this will make it easy to cherry pick the best ones to send.

There is also the option to go to graduate school online, which can be a real lifesaver for some. It alleviates the need to go to a campus, allowing students across the country and even the globe, to go to school virtually anywhere. The application process is almost identical to applying for a traditional program. Look into different degrees that interest you, some may be offered online. Take a close look at the length of the program, though. For example, UNH offered a one year compressed MBA program, which I completed. If I had done the online MBA program, it would have taken, at a minimum, two years to complete. With what I have seen, online program length depends heavily on the school. Some tend to space out courses more and require you to take less at a time, making the program longer. Instead of taking four in person classes per semester, you may only take two courses per online semester. This is usually to allow people to work full time while getting their degree. If this is something that interests you, online grad school may be your ticket to success!

There are some huge pros to going online for a graduate degree. First, obviously more choices of where to attend without having to physically relocate. As mentioned earlier, it's easier to have a full time job while attending school. You can also expect to enjoy lower costs for online programs.

It's likely cheaper for the same degree to be completed online. There are fewer costs for online programs than in person programs. Online graduate school is certainly something you should look into, you may be surprised to find it's a great option. But college and graduate school are just the beginning for you. You have so much potential and these first few years can set you up for a lifetime of success.

BEFORE THE FINAL CHAPTER...

Before we get into the final chapter, I need you to turn back to the beginning of the book to see what you wrote for questions, concerns, worries, and other thoughts. You will realize you now have so many more tools in your toolbox. After you turn to the front and take a look, come on back.

Welcome back! I want you to take the space below and write yourself some reminders. Things this book has taught you, things you need to remember when you head to school, things you'll want to look back on to give you confidence or that you're a badass and college has nothing on you.

_____

_____

_____

_____

_____

_____

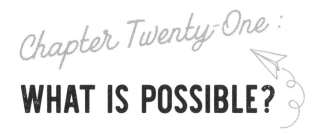

Chapter Twenty-One:
WHAT IS POSSIBLE?

" DON'T LET SOMEONE ELSE'S OPINION OF YOU BECOME YOUR REALITY. "

–LES BROWN

Before we enter this final section of the book, I would like to extend my sincerest gratitude for you taking your time to read about my experience and the tips, tricks, and tools I learned along the way. My mission in writing this book is to provide a resource for anyone thinking of going to college. There is a lot to figure out and I am extremely grateful to have the opportunity to assist you along your path. Enjoy this final section, and thank you for reading.

Each one of us will have a different life experience, which is one thing that makes life beautiful. I truly believe greatness lives in each and every-one of us, you just need to find it. So, what is possible for you in this life?

If you're reading this, you're able to take oxygen into your lungs and you're alive. If you're alive, anything is possible. People have come from nothing to build billion dollar businesses, run over 200 miles at once, score their dream job, become a professional athlete. Whatever you see for yourself, whether it's being a billionaire or being the best baker in your small town, you can do it. You need to make the decision within yourself what you're going to do and how you're going to get there, that's really it. There are endless success stories of people coming from a variety of backgrounds, they've all gone on to do incredible things throughout the world. Why not be one of those successes?

Everything is impossible until it's not.

You, as a tiny part of this universe, can make the world a better place. One way to start is to better yourself. If you are a better person, the world becomes better automatically. See potential within yourself, don't make excuses, and get after it. One thing many people don't think about is that they *deserve* to be happy. This is important here. Say this to yourself three times outloud, I challenge you. "I deserve to be happy!" Yeah, there you go! You deserve it, but one catch is that you are absolutely in charge of being happy, whatever happiness is to you. Being a human being and having the power of choice is what sets us apart as a species. Life is going to throw a lot at you, and how you *choose* to respond will determine your destiny. Take responsibility for the decisions you make, and know that in any situation you can decide to see the positive side, no matter how grim.

Even before this book you had all you needed. You're unstoppable.

You have come a long way on your journey through this book. There is a lot of information jam packed into just a few pages, please refer to this resource often if there is value in it for you. Similar to reading this resourceful book, you need to find resources that help you in whatever phase of life you happen to be in as well. I believe that resourcefulness *is* the ultimate resource; if you believe you can find the resources no matter what, you have all that you need. Seek to be resourceful, and I don't mean just in school, but in *life*. College is just a short part of your life, but it has the potential to be so impactful on your future. You'll endure experiences that'll change you forever. Don't be scared by that, though. Make the choices you know you should make, work like hell, and I truly believe you will end up right where you want to be. Enjoy this crazy ride we call life.

Thank YOU for investing your time into this bit of information, I hope it has had a positive impact on you. So, get out there, give it all you've got, and let me leave you with this:

"FEEL THE FEAR, AND DO IT ANYWAYS."

-SUSAN JEFFERS

CPSIA information can be obtained
at www.ICGtesting.com
Printed in the USA
BVHW051007100621
609275BV00011B/2312